SUSAN JUNG

# A
# CELEBRATION
## OF FOOD

First Printing, 2012
Printed in Hong Kong

ISBN 978-962-8148-08-0

Address permission requests to:

SCMP Strategic Marketing
South China Morning Post Publishers Limited
Morning Post Centre
22 Dai Fat Street
Tai Po Industrial Estate
New Territories
Hong Kong
www.scmp.com

Susan Jung is the author of this book.

BOOK DESIGN
Steve Ellul

FOOD STYLISTS
Nellie Ming Lee, Vivian Herijanto, Rachel Macchiesi

PHOTOGRAPHY:
Jason Joseph Bonello: Susan Jung's portrait and all chef and restaurant photos, plus pages 137 and 167
Patrick Poon - Koji Studio: pages 17, 21-23, 29, 37, 55-59, 71, 73, 85, 97, 107, 113, 121, 155, 171, 175
Jonathan Wong: cover photo and all other photos, other than pages 103, 131, 165 (KY Cheng) and 41 and 77 (Nora Tam)

SUSAN JUNG

# A
# CELEBRATION
## OF FOOD

"Susan Jung has distilled her passion for food in this book filled with easy, clear and mouth-watering recipes. Her wide experience as Food Editor is evident on every page of a book that belongs on every great cook's shelf."

Ken Hom, BBC-TV presenter and best-selling author

"Susan Jung is an inspiration: not only is she a serious restaurant critic, but as a chef herself she deeply understands food, textures, the marriage of ingredients and how to create fantastic dishes. This carefully compiled selection of must-try recipes will encourage everyone to pick up a pan and recreate them for friends, family and loved ones."

Uwe Opocensky, Executive Chef, Mandarin Oriental, Hong Kong

"Susan Jung has produced a mouthwatering collection of favourite recipes from her 15 years as Food Editor of the *South China Morning Post*. Clearly written and gorgeously illustrated, *A Celebration of Food* offers a thrilling glimpse of the diversity of Hong Kong cooking."

Fuchsia Dunlop, food writer and cookbook author specialising in Chinese cuisine

# CONT

**09** INTRODUCTION

## FAMILY

**12** SHAKSHUKA

**14** AEBLESKIVERS

**16** PAN-FRIED BUNS FILLED WITH PORK AND CHIVES

**18** ROASTED KABOCHA SOUP WITH GINGER AND CURRY

**20** ALBONDIGAS SOUP

**22** SAVOURY TONG YUEN

**24** WATERMELON, TOMATO AND FETA OR GOAT CHEESE SALAD

**26** BALINESE CHOPPED PURPLE CABBAGE AND CHICKEN SALAD

**28** SPINACH AND GARLIC SHRIMP SALAD

**30** CABBAGE KIMCHI

**32** STIR-FRIED LETTUCE WITH SHRIMP PASTE IN CLAY POT

**34** BRAISED POMELO SKIN WITH SHRIMP ROE

**36** FRITTO MISTO

**38** POLENTA WITH BACON, SHRIMP AND CHIVES

**40** STIR-FRIED RICE VERMICELLI WITH BELACAN, PORK BELLY AND SHRIMP

**42** MUSSELS WITH POTATOES, PEPPERS AND ROUILLE

**44** CHICKEN KARAAGE

**46** THAI-STYLE CHICKEN WINGS

**48** YELLOW EARTH CHICKEN

**50** TORTAS WITH SPICED FLANK STEAK, CRUSHED BLACK BEANS AND AVOCADO

**52** MAPO DOUFU

**54** HONEYCOMB TRIPE WITH PARMESAN CHEESE

**56** OXTAIL BRAISED IN RED WINE

**58** MACCHIESI FAMILY SPAGHETTI WITH POLPETTI

**60** CHINESE ALMOND SOUP

**62** SUMMER PUDDING

**64** BREAD PUDDING WITH CRÈME ANGLAISE AND WHISKY SAUCE

## FRIENDS

**68** FOCACCIA WITH PANCETTA, CARAMELISED ONIONS AND ROSEMARY

**70** CHICKPEAS WITH KABOCHA, CURRY AND YOGURT

**72** GRILLED QUAILS WITH BABY SPINACH, ARUGULA, BEETROOT AND MUSTARD DRESSING

**74** SLICED PORK WITH CHILLI AND GARLIC SAUCE

**76** CHERRY TOMATO AND RICOTTA TART WITH WHOLE-WHEAT AND OLIVE-OIL CRUST

**78** KIMCHI PANCAKES

**80** OCTOPUS CARPACCIO WITH OLIVE OIL, STICKY BALSAMIC AND SWEET PAPRIKA

**82** CURRY-DUSTED SHRIMP AND SCALLOP SKEWERS WITH MANGO, COCONUT AND KAFFIR LIME SALSA

**84** GRILLED BAMBOO CLAMS WITH GARLIC, BUTTER AND PARSLEY

**86** SAUTÉED SLICED ABALONE WITH ONION AND WILD MUSHROOMS

**88** SEARED TUNA WITH CORN, AVOCADO SALSA AND IKURA

**90** NASI LEMAK WITH SPICY PRAWNS

**92** ANGEL HAIR PASTA WITH UNI, TOMATOES AND GARLIC CHIPS

**94** SALT-BAKED FISH WITH UNI ROUILLE

**96** SCOTCH EGGS

**98** PORK SCHNITZEL WITH POTATO SALAD

**100** SPARE RIBS WITH PRESERVED PLUMS AND CARAMELISED BLACK VINEGAR

**102** CHOUCROUTE GARNIE

# ENTS

104 VIETNAMESE FRIED SPRING ROLLS

106 SPIRAL CURRY PUFFS

108 PIGEONS WITH GREEN PEAS, MORELS, BUTTER-ROASTED JAPANESE SWEET POTATOES AND BABY TARO

110 SMOKED CHICKEN

112 YUKHOE

114 RASPBERRY, VANILLA-POACHED APRICOT AND GREEK YOGURT PARFAITS WITH LEMON AND MUSCOVADO SUGAR CRUMBLE

116 BANANA CREAM PIE

118 AFFOGATO

120 CHOCOLATE AND SALTED CARAMEL TARTS

122 DEEP-DISH CHERRY PIE WITH FLAKY CRUST

## FEASTS

126 XO SAUCE

128 CHAWANMUSHI WITH BLACK TRUFFLE PASTE AND UNI

130 MUSHROOM SOUP WITH TRUFFLE OIL AND MUSHROOM TOAST

132 AJO BLANCO WITH GRAPE SORBET AND CROUTONS

134 HEIRLOOM BEETS WITH YOGURT AND CREAM CHEESE ESPUMA

136 SOFT-SHELL CRAB SALAD WITH CANDIED ORANGE PEEL, TOASTED HAZELNUTS AND CITRUS DRESSING

138 SNAPPER WITH BABY SPINACH

140 CITRUS, FENNEL AND AQUAVIT-CURED SALMON WITH LEMON-HORSERADISH SOUR CREAM

142 CRAB TIRAMISU WITH FRUIT AND TANDOORI SPICES

144 CRAB, ASPARAGUS AND SAFFRON TARTS

146 OOLONG TEA-SMOKED DUCK EGGS WITH BLACK TRUFFLE PASTE

148 MISO-MARINATED BLACK COD IN HOBA LEAF WITH PICKLED YOUNG JAPANESE GINGER

150 SALT-ROASTED LANGOUSTINES WITH ROASTED CHERRY TOMATOES, WHITE WINE, ARUGULA AND SQUID-INK PASTA

152 PIPA DOUFU

154 NOR MAI GAI

156 QUAILS WITH ROASTED GARLIC, CARAMELISED LEMON, PETITS POIS AND CARROTS

158 VEAL SWEETBREADS WITH BEURRE NOISETTE AND CAPERS

160 SALTED CARAMEL ICE-CREAM SUNDAES WITH BITTERSWEET CHOCOLATE SAUCE AND SWEET AND SALTY POPCORN

162 KOUIGN AMANN

164 PINEAPPLE TARTS

166 MACARONS WITH SAKURA CREAM

168 ALAIN DUCASSE'S FINANCIERS

170 CHAMPAGNE SABAYON WITH FRESH BERRIES

172 GINGERBREAD PEOPLE

174 CHOCOLATE BUTTER CRUNCH

176 ACKNOWLEDGEMENTS

178 INDEX

# INTRODUCTION

wasn't always aware of my interest in food. But looking back at my childhood in Monterey Park, California, I showed signs from a young age that I liked to eat. When I read the fairy tale *Rapunzel*, it didn't make me wish for a prince who would rescue me; instead, I wondered what plant could be so delicious that it would make a woman send her husband over a wall to steal it from a witch's garden. When I was about 10, I read Sylvia Plath's *The Bell Jar*, but it wasn't until I studied the book in high school that I realised it was about a young woman going mad. All I remembered from my childhood reading was the luncheon party scene during which the protagonist eats two whole bowls of caviar.

Fortunately, I grew up in a family that loved food. Both my parents are good cooks and my Ah Ma (paternal grandmother) even more so. With the help of my father, she would make dinner every Saturday and lunch on Sunday for at least 20 people. On holidays, friends and the entire family (my paternal grandparents, their eight children and spouses, plus 23 grandchildren) would get together for one of her feasts. My globe-trotting uncle Gene, who

could sample a dish and figure out how to make it, introduced us to exotic fare such as bisteeya (Moroccan savoury-sweet pigeon pie) and paté en croute.

When I left home to read English Literature at UC Berkeley, I became homesick for the Chinese dishes my mother and grandmother made. Over the phone, my mother instructed me to marinate meats in "a little soy sauce, rice wine, salt, sugar, cornstarch …" I made horrendous renditions of her dishes until I learned how much "a little" was and became adept at Chinese home-style cooking. Between writing papers and studying for exams, I pored over cookbooks and attempted complicated, time-consuming recipes such as lobster bisque and veal demi-glace.

After graduating, I made lavish meals for friends while trying to muster the energy to apply to journalism school. But then a friend said, "Since you like to cook so much, why don't you do it professionally?"

Excellent advice. Purely out of vanity (I didn't want to smell of garlic), I decided to specialise in pastry. My skills took me from San Francisco to New York to Hong Kong, where I had been offered a job as a pastry chef. After working

at several restaurants here, I started writing freelance articles for the *South China Morning Post*. Then features editor Charles Anderson offered me a full-time job, and on July 1, 1997, the day of Hong Kong's handover to China, I became the SCMP's Food and Wine Editor.

I still have a hard time believing I have a job that allows me to think about food as much as I want to without being accused of wasting time. I've interviewed famous chefs and eaten delicious meals everywhere from roadside stalls in Vietnam to restaurants in Spain that required bookings six months in advance. I've also created and tested recipes for the *Post Magazine* column on which this cookbook is based.

If just a little of my enthusiasm for food comes across in my writing, I consider that to be a success.

*Susan Jung*

SUSAN JUNG 2012

FA

# MILY

For the most part, the recipes in this chapter make for easy weekday meals, although the few that require long simmering might be better kept for leisurely weekend dinners. The simple techniques and easily available ingredients, however, do not make these dishes any less delicious.

# SHAKSHUKA

When I told my friend Celine that I was making shakshuka for this photoshoot, she said, "I hope you're using the [Yotam] Ottolenghi recipe."

I had been thinking of using that recipe, from the Israeli-born chef's book *Plenty*, so asked Celine if it was good. She replied, "It's fantastic, you don't need to change a thing." I ended up changing it a tiny bit - I added fresh chilli, piment d'Espelette and feta, and adapted the cooking method slightly but I agree with her that it's a delicious recipe from an excellent book.

## INGREDIENTS

1/4 tsp whole cumin seeds
About 150ml olive oil, divided
2 large onions, sliced about 3mm thick
2 red bell peppers
2 yellow bell peppers
1-2 hot green chillies, or more to taste
5-10 grams brown sugar
2 bay leaves
6 small thyme sprigs
2 tbsp chopped parsley
2 tbsp chopped coriander, plus whole leaves for the garnish
1/2 tsp saffron threads
1/2 tsp piment d'Espelette, or to taste
750 grams red cherry tomatoes, halved
Fine sea salt and freshly ground black pepper
4-6 large free-range eggs
100-150 grams feta cheese

## METHOD

1 Cut off the stem and bottom ends of the red and yellow peppers. Remove and discard the core and seeds, then cut the peppers into 5mm-wide strips. Cut the chillies into rounds about 5mm thick (if you want the dish to be less hot, remove the seeds).

2 Heat a dry (unoiled) skillet (preferably cast iron) over a medium flame, add the cumin seeds and stir constantly until fragrant and toasted. Add about 100ml of the olive oil to the pan, stir in the onion and cook over a medium flame until the onion slices are wilted. Add the red and yellow peppers, chillies, sugar, bay leaves, thyme sprigs, chopped parsley and coriander, and the saffron and piment d'Espelette, then season to taste with salt. Add more oil to the skillet so the ingredients are well coated, then continue to cook for about five minutes, stirring often. Stir in the tomatoes, bring to the boil, lower the heat and simmer, stirring occasionally, until the tomatoes are very soft. If too much liquid evaporates, stir in some water. The consistency should be slightly soupy. The dish can be made in advance to this point and refrigerated; when needed, reheat the mixture until simmering.

3 Ladle the hot shakshuka into four to six shallow, individual-sized serving dishes that can be used on the stovetop. Crack an egg into each portion and crumble the cheese on top. Put the lids on the dishes (or if they don't have lids, cover them tightly with aluminium foil), then simmer them on the stovetop for several minutes or until the eggs are cooked. Garnish with fresh coriander, sprinkle with pepper and serve with warm, crusty bread.

Serves 4-6.

# AEBLESKIVERS

To make these, you need a special pan with half-sphere indentations. I've never seen an aebleskiver pan in Hong Kong so I use an inexpensive cast-iron pan made for takoyaki (Japanese octopus balls), which are cooked in a similar way to aebleskivers. You can buy the pan at shops specialising in Japanese household products, such as Apita in Taikoo Shing and Sogo in Causeway Bay.

The cooking technique described below sounds much more difficult than it is. Your first attempts might not yield perfectly round balls (although the aebleskivers will still be edible) but they will improve quickly with practice. It might take a little time to figure out how your stovetop heats the pan - on mine, the batter browns much more quickly in the centre indentations, so once the aebleskivers become firm, I move the ones in the middle to the outside indentations and vice versa so they all brown and cook evenly.

This recipe is based on one from the eGullet website.

## INGREDIENTS

250 grams plain (all-purpose) flour
1/2 tsp ground cardamom (optional)
25 grams sugar
1/2 tsp fine sea salt
3 large eggs, at room temperature
450ml whole milk
8 grams active dry yeast
30 grams unsalted butter, melted and cooled to lukewarm
Cooking oil, for greasing the pan
Icing sugar, for dusting
Fruit preserves, for serving (I use strawberry or raspberry jam)

## METHOD

1 Heat the milk to simmering then cool to 35 degrees Celsius. Stir the yeast into the milk and let it stand for five minutes. In a bowl, whisk the flour with the cardamom, sugar and salt. Whisk together the eggs, milk/yeast mixture and butter, pour over the flour and combine - the mixture will be slightly lumpy. Leave at room temperature for about an hour. The mixture can be used immediately or covered with cling film and refrigerated for up to a day. If you refrigerate the batter (it should be stirred periodically), let it stand at room temperature for about 30 minutes before using. Stir the batter before transferring it to a measuring cup with a pouring spout.

2 Heat an aebleskiver pan over a medium flame, then lightly coat each indentation with oil. Stir the batter, then pour some of it into each indentation to fill it almost completely. Leave for about 45 seconds, or until the bottom sets. Use a small fork or a wooden skewer to give the aebleskiver a quarter "turn" so the batter in the centre flows out into the pan. Cook to set the bottom, then give it another turn so more batter flows out of the centre into the pan and the first cooked side is on top. You'll need to give each aebleskiver two or three partial turns - if you just flip it over only once, the aebleskiver will collapse slightly and be an ellipse, rather than a ball.

3 Once it is set, brown the bottom and set the interior, then flip it over to brown the other side, adjusting the heat if they brown too quickly or slowly. Stir the batter and coat the pan with oil before cooking each batch. For each portion, put three aebleskivers on a plate, dust with icing sugar and serve with a spoonful of jam.

Makes 25-30.

# PAN-FRIED BUNS FILLED WITH PORK AND CHIVES

Be sure to use the slim, flat, dark green variety of Chinese chives (sometimes called Chinese leeks), not the tubular, tougher, flowering garlic chives. The secret to a juicy filling is a rich gelatinous broth that's solid when cold - the heat from cooking the buns turns the broth to liquid again. Slowly simmer 80ml of home-made chicken, pork or vegetable stock with a 6cm x 6cm piece of fresh pig skin in a covered pan until the skin is tender. Remove and discard the skin and let the liquid cool before mixing it with the other filling ingredients.

## INGREDIENTS

FOR THE DOUGH
**450 grams plain (all-purpose) flour**
**240ml boiling water**

FOR THE FILLING
**500 grams minced pork**
**80 grams finely minced Chinese chives**
**5 grams finely minced ginger**
**20ml soy sauce**
**5ml sesame oil**
**10ml rice wine**
**1/4 tsp fine sea salt**
**1/2 tsp sugar**
**A pinch of ground white pepper**
**80ml of pig skin-enriched chicken, pork or vegetable stock**

FOR THE DIPPING SAUCE
**Chinese brown vinegar**
**Soy sauce**
**Chilli paste**

## METHOD

**1** Thoroughly mix all the filling ingredients and chill in the fridge for several hours.

**2** Place the flour in a bowl, add 200ml of boiling water and stir with a wooden spoon. If the mixture seems dry, add more water. When the dough is cool enough to handle, knead it until it's smooth and neither sticky nor dry. Let it rest for at least 30 minutes. Roll into a snake and cut into 20 to 24 even pieces. Shape each piece into a ball, flatten and stretch it with your fingers until it's about 10cm in diameter, slightly thicker at the centre and very thin at the edges. Scoop a spoonful of the cold filling into the centre of the disc of dough - you want to stuff it as fully as possible without making any holes in the wrapper. Stretch the dough over the filling and firmly pinch the seams to seal it into a round ball, then flatten gently, seam-side down, so it's about 6cm in diameter. Place the buns on a lightly oiled pan, cover with a lightly oiled piece of cling film, then chill them for 30 minutes.

**3** Heat a skillet and liberally coat it with oil. Put in enough buns so they're touching but not crowded (you'll need to cook them in batches). Pan-fry seam side-down over a medium flame until lightly browned, then turn them over and brown the other side. Flip the buns over again, cover and turn the heat to medium-low. Cook for about five minutes, flipping once. Serve hot. The dipping sauce can be mixed to individual tastes.

Makes 20-24.

# ROASTED KABOCHA SOUP WITH GINGER AND CURRY

Kabocha is a Japanese squash with a hard green rind and mildly sweet, bright orange flesh. You can substitute it with other types of winter squash such as sugar pumpkin, acorn or butternut squash.

## INGREDIENTS

About 30ml olive oil, divided, plus more for brushing and pan-frying the croutons
900 grams kabocha, seeds removed
15 grams unsalted butter
30-50 grams fresh ginger, finely minced
4-5 shallots, minced
3/4 tsp curry powder, or to taste
675ml unsalted chicken stock (home-made if possible)
45ml coconut milk
Fine sea salt and freshly ground black pepper
4 to 6 baguette slices, cut about 8mm thick on the diagonal
Freshly grated parmesan, for sprinkling

## METHOD

1 Preheat the oven to 180 degrees Celsius. Cut the kabocha into thick wedges, drizzle lightly with olive oil and sprinkle with salt and pepper. Cook at 180 degrees until tender (about 45 minutes). Allow to cool, then scoop the squash from the rind.

2 Pour 15ml of olive oil into a saucepan, add the butter and heat over a medium flame until melted. Add the ginger and shallots and cook, stirring often, until the shallots are translucent. Add the curry powder and stir constantly for about one minute. Add the kabocha, chicken stock and salt and pepper. Bring to a simmer, then cook over a medium-low flame for about 10 minutes. Purée the soup until smooth, then pour back into the pan and add the coconut milk. If the soup is too thick, stir in some water. Heat until simmering and taste for seasoning.

3 Lightly brush the cut surfaces of the baguette slices with olive oil. Sprinkle some parmesan evenly over one side of each slice and press it in firmly so it adheres. Heat olive oil to a depth of about 3mm in a skillet and when it's hot, pan-fry the baguette slices over a medium flame until toasted on each side. Ladle the soup into bowls and drizzle a little olive oil over it. Add a crouton to each bowl and serve immediately.

Serves 4-6.

# ALBONDIGAS SOUP

This recipe is adapted from one in Diana Kennedy's book *Nothing Fancy*.

## INGREDIENTS

FOR THE MEATBALLS

**15 grams raw long-grain rice**
**180 grams minced pork**
**180 grams minced beef**
**1 small egg, beaten**
**1/8 tsp ground cumin**
**3 large fresh mint leaves, finely chopped**
**1/4 tsp dried oregano**
**50 grams white onion, minced**
**Fine sea salt and freshly ground black pepper, to taste**

FOR THE SOUP

**15ml cooking oil**
**1 large shallot, minced**
**1 large garlic clove, minced**
**450 grams canned Italian tomato puree**
**180 grams carrots, cut into 5mm cubes**
**180 grams small zucchini, halved lengthwise and cut on the diagonal into 5mm slices**
**500ml chicken or vegetable stock**
**Fresh green chillies, finely chopped, to taste**
**Fresh coriander leaves**

## METHOD

**1** Pour boiling water over the rice, leave for 30 minutes and drain. Combine the pork and beef with the rice, egg, cumin, mint, oregano, onion and salt and pepper.

**2** Shape the mixture into balls about 1.5cm in diameter, place them on a tray lined with cling film and refrigerate for an hour.

**3** Heat the oil in a soup pot, add the shallot and garlic, then cook until soft. Add the tomato puree and stir over a high heat for about two minutes. Add the carrot, zucchini, stock, chillies, salt and pepper and 1 litre of water. Bring to the simmer and add the meatballs. Lower the heat and simmer for about 45 minutes.

Taste for seasoning and add fresh coriander leaves just before serving.

Serves about 4.

# SAVOURY TONG YUEN

I had never tasted sweet tong yuen until I moved to Hong Kong because my family in California ate them in savoury soup. This recipe comes from my favourite uncle, who taught it to my mother. We always made tong yuen and meatballs quite small, which is time-consuming, but they can be larger if you prefer. Chung choi is salted turnip green. They come in little bundles and should be unrolled and rinsed well to wash off excess salt.

## INGREDIENTS

FOR THE TONG YUEN
**200 grams glutinous rice flour**
**About 150ml hot water**

FOR THE PORK BALLS
**500 grams minced pork**
**1 small piece chung choi, rinsed well**
**2 spring onions**
**20ml soy sauce**
**10ml rice wine**
**1/2 tsp sugar**
**1/4 tsp salt**
**1/4 tsp finely ground white pepper**
**10ml sesame oil**
**2 tsp cornstarch**

FOR THE SOUP
**15ml cooking oil**
**40 grams dried shrimp, soaked in about 200ml warm water for at least an hour**
**1/2 tsp salt**
**4-5 slices (about 2mm thick) ginger, peeled**
**About 500 grams Chinese radish (loh bak)**
**400ml chicken stock**
**15ml soy sauce**
**Sesame oil**
**Chopped spring onions, fresh coriander leaves**

## METHOD

**1** To make the tong yuen, put the glutinous rice flour in a bowl and add the hot water. Stir with a pair of chopsticks to form a thick mass. If the mixture is dry, drizzle in a little more hot water. As soon as the dough is cool enough to handle, knead it until it's smooth and not sticky. It should be pliable, but firm enough to hold its shape.

**2** Take a portion of the dough (cover the rest with plastic wrap) and shape into a log. Cut the log into smaller pieces, then roll each one into a ball about 1cm in diameter. Place the balls on a tray or plate lined with plastic wrap. Don't let them touch each other or they'll stick together. Shape the remaining dough.

**3** Heat a large pot of salted water and, when it's boiling, add the tong yuen. Cook them in batches if necessary. The tong yuen are ready when they float to the surface. Scoop them out of the water with a sieve or slotted spoon and place in a bowl of cool water.

**4** To make the pork balls, chop the chung choi and spring onions and add them to the minced pork. Add the soy sauce, rice wine, sugar, salt, white pepper, cornstarch and sesame oil and mix thoroughly. Shape into balls about 1.5cm in diameter.

**5** Cut the loh bak into thick matchstick strips about 3cm long. Julienne the ginger. Drain the shrimp but reserve the soaking liquid. Heat the oil in a large pot and add the dried shrimp, shredded ginger and salt. Stir-fry for about 30 seconds, then add the chicken broth, the shrimp soaking liquid, 15ml soy sauce and about 1 litre of cold water. Bring to the boil and add the pork balls. Reduce the heat and simmer for about two minutes. Add the loh bak and simmer until tender and translucent. Drain the cooked tong yuen, add them to the pot and simmer to heat through (about two minutes). Taste for seasonings then ladle into bowls, drizzle with sesame oil and add the coriander and chopped spring onions.

Serves about 6.

# WATERMELON, TOMATO AND FETA OR GOAT CHEESE SALAD

The combination of sweet fruit with savoury protein is common in Mediterranean countries: think of melon or figs with Parma ham, and fresh tomatoes with mozzarella cheese, a classic in Italy. Many countries can lay claim to this refreshing salad of watermelon with tomato and cheese. It should be served very cold - keep the ingredients in the fridge and mix in the vinaigrette just before serving.

## INGREDIENTS

600 grams chilled watermelon, with the rind removed (weigh it after cutting off the rind)
175 grams red and yellow cherry tomatoes, halved
150 grams feta or goats' cheese
20ml aged balsamic vinegar
10ml rice vinegar
10ml pure sesame oil, or to taste
40ml extra virgin olive oil
Fine sea salt and freshly ground black pepper, to taste
Rough-flaked sea salt (such as Maldon)

## METHOD

1 In a small bowl, whisk the balsamic vinegar with the rice vinegar. Whisking constantly, drizzle in the sesame oil and extra virgin olive oil. Sprinkle in pepper and just a little fine sea salt (the cheese is salty). Check the seasoning by dipping a cherry tomato in the vinaigrette and tasting it - add a little more sesame oil, if needed (you should be able to taste the sesame oil but it shouldn't be overwhelming).

2 Cut the watermelon into two-bite chunks and mix with the cherry tomatoes. Chill in the fridge until ready to serve.

3 Just before serving, pour the vinaigrette over the watermelon and cherry tomatoes and mix. Cut the cheese into cubes, add to the watermelon and tomatoes, sprinkle with rough-flaked sea salt and mix gently.

Serves about 6.

# BALINESE CHOPPED PURPLE CABBAGE AND CHICKEN SALAD

Jakarta-born *Vivian Herijanto* grew up in Indonesia, Singapore and the United States. After graduating from Boston University with a BS in business administration, she attended the Institute of Culinary Education in New York, then worked at Jean-Georges Vongerichten's Spice Market. She moved to Hong Kong in 2004 and freelanced as a food stylist before opening Corner Kitchen Cooking School and Heirloom Eatery, both in Sheung Wan.

Herijanto says this salad, which has been one of Heirloom's most popular items since it opened in 2011, is a variation on the traditional Indonesian dish of karedok, which is similar to gado gado. Herijanto toned down the original dish's sweetness, replacing the peanut sauce with a dressing that's a little spicier.

## INGREDIENTS

4 chicken breasts, about 200 grams each
Cooking oil, for the skillet
1 head of purple cabbage, finely shredded
250 grams snake beans, blanched in boiling water, then sliced into 5mm pieces
100 grams cherry tomatoes, quartered lengthwise
1-2 ripe avocados
1 fresh lime

FOR THE DRESSING
1/2 tsp whole cumin seeds
1/2 tsp whole coriander seeds
1/2 tsp whole fennel seeds
1 red finger chilli, roughly chopped
3 garlic cloves, roughly chopped
3 large shallots, roughly chopped
50 grams fresh lemongrass, juicy core only, thinly sliced
2 lime leaves, torn into pieces
120ml vegetable oil
1 tbsp granulated sugar
30ml fresh lime juice, or to taste
30ml fresh lemon juice, or to taste
Fine sea salt and freshly ground black pepper

## METHOD

1 Butterfly the chicken breasts: cut them in half lengthwise, slicing parallel to the cutting board and leaving them intact by a seam of meat. Open the breasts like a book and season both sides with salt and pepper. Grill or pan-fry them in a lightly oiled pan until cooked through. Squeeze some lime juice on top and, when cool enough to handle, dice the breasts into 1cm cubes.

2 Toast the cumin, coriander and fennel seeds until fragrant, then pound them in a mortar when cool. Add the chilli, garlic, shallots, lemongrass and lime leaves and pound everything to a rough paste.

3 Heat the oil in a saucepan and add the sugar and pounded spice mixture. Cook over a low-medium flame, stirring often, until the ingredients are soft and slightly browned. Add the lime and lemon juices and season to taste with salt and pepper. Cool the mixture, then taste for seasonings and adjust if needed.

4 Peel and slice the avocados. Put the cabbage, snake beans, cherry tomatoes and chicken in a large bowl, add the dressing and mix thoroughly. Pile onto a plate, top with the avocado slices and serve.

Serves 6.

# SPINACH AND GARLIC SHRIMP SALAD

This recipe comes from Vivian Herijanto, who owns Heirloom restaurant, which is featured on page 26.

## INGREDIENTS

16 medium-sized shrimp (about 6cm, excluding the head)
120ml olive oil
6 large garlic cloves, peeled and thinly sliced lengthwise
1 tsp dried red chilli flakes
20ml sherry vinegar
140 grams baby spinach leaves
Half a lemon
Fine sea salt and freshly ground black pepper, to taste

## METHOD

1 Twist off the heads from the shrimp and use kitchen shears to cut off the legs. Use a sharp knife to split the shrimp down the back through the shell, then remove the dark vein. Rinse the shrimp under cold water, pat dry and season thoroughly with salt and pepper.

2 Heat the oil with the sliced garlic and chilli flakes in a skillet over a medium-high flame. When the garlic starts to colour slightly, add the shrimp and cook until the flesh turns opaque. Use a slotted spoon to remove the shrimp and garlic from the pan. Carefully add the sherry vinegar to the pan and whisk it with the oil and chilli flakes.

3 Scatter the spinach leaves on a large platter and drizzle with the dressing. Add the shrimp and the garlic. Squeeze lemon juice over the salad and serve immediately.

Serves 4 as a starter, 2 as a main course.

# CABBAGE KIMCHI

Change this recipe according to your tastes. Use less gochugaru (chilli flakes) if you like it less spicy and add other ingredients, such as fresh mustard leaf, julienned carrot, raw oysters or thinly sliced, raw cutlass fish. Be sure to use large, fat heads of Napa cabbage - they're sweeter and have a crisper bite than long, thin ones. For the same reason, you should also use fatter (in diameter) pieces of white radish.

   Most of the ingredients are available at the Korean shops on Kimberley Street in Tsim Sha Tsui. Be sure to wear plastic gloves when spreading the chilli paste on the cabbage leaves, or your hands will burn from the gochugaru.

   Kimchi keeps for weeks in the fridge. If it becomes too sour, it can be used to make cooked dishes such as kimchi pancakes (see recipe on page 78) or kimchi chigae.

## INGREDIENTS

2.5kg Napa cabbage
300 grams kosher or medium-flaked sea salt
35 grams sweet rice flour (also known as glutinous rice flour)
240ml water
About 50 grams plain sugar
100 grams gochugaru (use fine flakes, not the coarse ones)
100ml salted anchovy sauce
100 grams Korean salted shrimp, drained and chopped
40 grams minced garlic
20 grams grated ginger
300-500 grams white radish
80 grams flat Chinese chives, cut into 2cm lengths
80 grams spring onions, cut into 2cm lengths

## METHOD

1 Use a large knife to cut the head of the Napa cabbage through the base only, then use your hands to tear the head in half. Cut each half again through the base and tear it into two pieces. (Tearing it lets the leaves divide themselves naturally, so you end up with fewer small pieces.) Rinse the cabbage thoroughly, washing between the leaves, then drain and shake off the water. Sprinkle salt lightly over each leaf and more liberally at the base, where the leaves are thicker. Put the cabbage in a large bowl and leave for about three hours, turning the pieces over occasionally and pressing down on them as they soften. The cabbage is ready when the leaves are soft enough to squeeze without breaking. Drain the cabbage and rinse thoroughly between the leaves until the salt has been removed. Taste several pieces of the cabbage, which shouldn't be too salty. Squeeze out the excess water.

2 Put the rice flour in a small pan with the water and stir to a smooth paste. Heat over a medium-low flame and stir until simmering. Continue to stir until the mixture looks translucent, then stir in the sugar and remove from the heat. Cool the mixture, put it into a large bowl and add the gochugaru, anchovy sauce, shrimp, garlic, ginger and one tablespoon of salt. Peel the white radish, cut it into 2mm-thick matchsticks and add to the bowl. Add the chives and spring onions and mix all the ingredients thoroughly.

3 Wearing plastic gloves and working with one piece of cabbage at a time, spread the chilli mixture in a thin layer from the base to the tip of each leaf. When all the leaves have been covered, roll the cabbage in a tight ball from the stem part towards the tip. Take one of the outer leaves of the cabbage head and - leaving it intact at the base - wrap it as tightly as possible around the ball of kimchi, then place it in a clean glass jar. Do the same with the remaining chilli paste and cabbage. Scrape any remaining chilli paste into the container and cover with the lid. It can be eaten immediately or fermented in the fridge. While it's fermenting, occasionally open the jar and press down on the ingredients.

# STIR-FRIED LETTUCE WITH SHRIMP PASTE IN CLAY POT

Fan Tang, in Leighton Road, Causeway Bay, looks more like a private club than a restaurant. A "doorperson" sits outside the entrance, which bears a small, discreet sign, and checks the name of the reservation before pushing a button that opens the sliding door.

The impression that it's members only doesn't end when you're inside. The interior is tastefully and expensively furnished with plush, comfortable chairs and still-life oil paintings on the walls. The wealthy (and often famous) clientele expect discretion. In fact it's so private the manager, Alfa Chan, declines to identify Fan Tang's owner.

Despite the moneyed patrons the menu features such humble dishes as stir-fried lettuce with shrimp paste in clay pot. Chef *Tong Ho-cheung*, who's been at the restaurant since it opened in 2009, takes just two minutes to cook the dish in his powerful wok.

Be sure to leave enough time to pre-heat the clay pot so the ingredients sizzle when they're put in. And have all the ingredients at hand so they're ready to go into the wok at the right time.

## INGREDIENTS

1-2 garlic cloves, minced
1 shallot, minced
1-2 slices peeled ginger, finely julienned
A few slices mild red chilli
2-3 heads (about 10cm long) sang choi (Chinese lettuce), cut lengthwise through the stem into four pieces
1/2 tsp to 1 tsp shrimp paste, crumbled
2 tsp oil, plus extra for the wok
About 20ml yellow wine, plus extra for the pot
Sugar, to taste
Salt, to taste

## METHOD

1 Put the glazed clay pot, lid on, into the oven and set the temperature to 200 degrees Celsius. Heat the pot for 20 minutes.

2 Mix the shrimp paste with 2 tsp oil, the yellow wine and a little sugar and salt.

3 Lightly oil the wok and heat over a high flame. Add the garlic, shallot, ginger and chilli and stir-fry briefly. Add the sang choi and a splash of water and stir-fry for about a minute. Add the shrimp paste mixture and stir-fry very quickly until the lettuce is lightly coated in sauce but still crisp. Transfer the ingredients into the hot clay pot (they should sizzle). Put the lid on the pot and pour some yellow wine around the edge of the lid to create fragrant steam. Serve immediately.

Serves 4 as part of a Chinese meal.

Sudden temperature extremes may crack clay pots. Don't put the hot pot on a cool or wet surface. Place it on a mat that will absorb the heat.

# BRAISED POMELO SKIN WITH SHRIMP ROE

*Lai Yau-tim* cooked at the Hang Seng Bank headquarters for 33 years, working his way up through the ranks until he was the chef of the dining room for senior staff. In 2000 he opened Tim's Kitchen in a tiny space on Jervois Street, Sheung Wan. Although it was a no-frills eatery – with a bathroom that was best avoided – it soon had wealthy diners lining up for its classic Cantonese dishes. In 2007 Lai opened a branch in Macau and in 2010 he moved the original restaurant into two-storey premises in nearby Bonham Strand.

Although Lai no longer works nightly at his restaurants, he is hands-on in the operation, assisted by his son, *Maurice* (right, with Lai), who cooks at home only, not in the restaurant. Tim's Kitchen's famous dishes include braised whole crab claw with winter melon, fried chicken, snake bisque and traditional Cantonese braised pomelo skin with shrimp roe. Lai uses baby pomelos, which he imports from Thailand, to make the dish because, he says, they have a proportionately thicker skin than fully grown pomelos and, when cooked, are more succulent.

## INGREDIENTS

**The skin from one baby pomelo, removed in two large pieces**
**Oil, as needed**

FOR THE BRAISING LIQUID
**400 grams fresh dace fish, cut into two pieces**
**30ml rice wine**
**20 grams dried Chinese ham, cut into small cubes**
**25 grams dried sole fish**
**25 grams dried shrimp**
**10 grams dried scallops, broken into pieces**
**200ml light, homemade chicken stock**
**600ml water**
**Fine sea salt, to taste**

TO FINISH THE DISH
**1 heaped tsp shrimp roe that's been mixed with oil, spring onion and ginger, then steamed for one hour (large quantities can be made in advance and refrigerated)**
**About 200ml light, homemade chicken stock**
**Oyster sauce, to taste**
**Sesame oil, to taste**
**Cornstarch dissolved in water, as needed**

## METHOD

1 Scrape off and discard the zest from the pomelo skin. Bring a pot of water to the boil, add the pomelo skin and simmer for a few minutes. Put the pieces in cool water and soak for at least an hour. Squeeze out the water, rinse with fresh water and squeeze again. Repeat the blanching, soaking and squeezing process once more. This can be done in advance.

2 Make the braising liquid. Lightly coat a wok with oil and heat over a high flame. Put the fresh dace in the wok and press on it so the skin is seared. Flip the pieces over and sear the other side. Add the rice wine, the Chinese ham and dried seafood, then stir in the chicken stock and the water. Bring to the boil, lower the heat and simmer for about 20 minutes. Skim off the foam and season with salt. Put the stock (with all the solid ingredients) in a large clay pot. Place a loosely woven bamboo net over the ingredients. Fill a bowl with oil. Squeeze the pomelo skin to extract excess water, then put the pieces in the bowl of oil and soak until they're saturated. Place the pieces on the bamboo net, cover with another bamboo net and invert a plate over the net to weigh down the pomelo peel so it is submerged in the liquid. Bring to the boil, cover with the lid and cook on a low simmer for two hours. Remove the pomelo skin from the stock.

3 Finish the dish by heating the chicken stock with shrimp roe, oyster sauce and sesame oil. Stir in some cornstarch dissolved in water to thicken the sauce to a light coating consistency. Heat the pomelo skin in the liquid and transfer to a shallow serving dish. Ladle the sauce over the top and serve.

Serves 4 as part of a Chinese meal.

The braising liquid is enough to make 20 portions of this dish; it can be strained and frozen for later use.
The chefs prepare the pomelo skin in advance, stopping after they braise the pieces in the stock. Each segment of peel is then wrapped individually in two layers of cling film and frozen. The dish is heated and sauced to order.

# FRITTO MISTO

The following seafood and vegetables are just suggestions; use whatever looks best in the market (small whole fish are a good addition). Take care when frying squid because it splatters more than many other types of seafood. Larger squids take less time to clean than the smaller ones, but it's not a job for the squeamish.

I like to buy very small shrimp (about 4cm, including the head) and cook them whole (just snip off the antennae). The shells are so thin and delicate that frying renders them crisp and edible and, of course, the heads are full of delicious juices. If you want to peel them first, buy the larger varieties because it's time-consuming to peel so many small shrimp.

Have your guests waiting at the table and serve the food as soon as it's fried.

## INGREDIENTS

**About 800 grams fresh squid**
**About 750 grams fresh shrimp**
**2 medium fennel bulbs**
**2 packs enoki mushrooms**
**200 grams thin asparagus**
**2 red peppers, stems and cores discarded, cut into 1cm wide strips**
**Cooking oil, for frying**

FOR THE BATTER
**120 grams cornstarch**
**200 grams plain flour**
**Approximately 500 grams cold sparkling water**
**Fine-flaked sea salt and freshly ground black pepper**
**Lemon wedges, for serving**

## METHOD

**1** Make the batter. Combine the cornstarch, flour and salt and pepper. Whisk in about 350ml cold water until smooth. Test the consistency by dipping your finger in the batter - it should lightly coat it. If it's too thick, whisk in more water. Cover and refrigerate for about two hours.

**2** Clean the squid by pulling off the heads and pulling out the innards (if they're large, you can slit them down one side and scrape out the insides). Pull out the transparent "quill" and any remaining guts, then peel off the tough purple skin. Wash the bodies under running water. If they're small squid, cut the bodies into rings. If they're large, lightly score the bodies in a diamond pattern and cut into strips about 8cm long and 2cm wide. Cut off and discard the face, leaving only the tentacles.

If using small shrimp, snip off the antennae. Remove the heads and shells of larger shrimp.

**3** Discard the fronds, tough fibres and cores of the fennel bulbs, then slice to a thickness of about 5mm. Simmer in salted water for about two minutes. Pat dry with paper towels. Discard the brown ends of the enoki stem and divide the mushrooms into smaller clumps (the exact size doesn't matter).

**4** Pour oil into a pan to a depth of about 8cm. Heat to 170 degrees Celsius. Dip the ingredients, including the asparagus and peppers, into the batter and fry to cook through: how long depends on the ingredients (the seafood and enoki take less time). Do not crowd the pan. Drain on paper towels. When everything is fried, turn up the heat to 180 degrees Celsius and fry the pieces a second time for about 30 seconds (this is to crisp the batter - it will remain pale-coloured). Drain on paper towels and serve immediately with lemon wedges.

Serves 4-6.

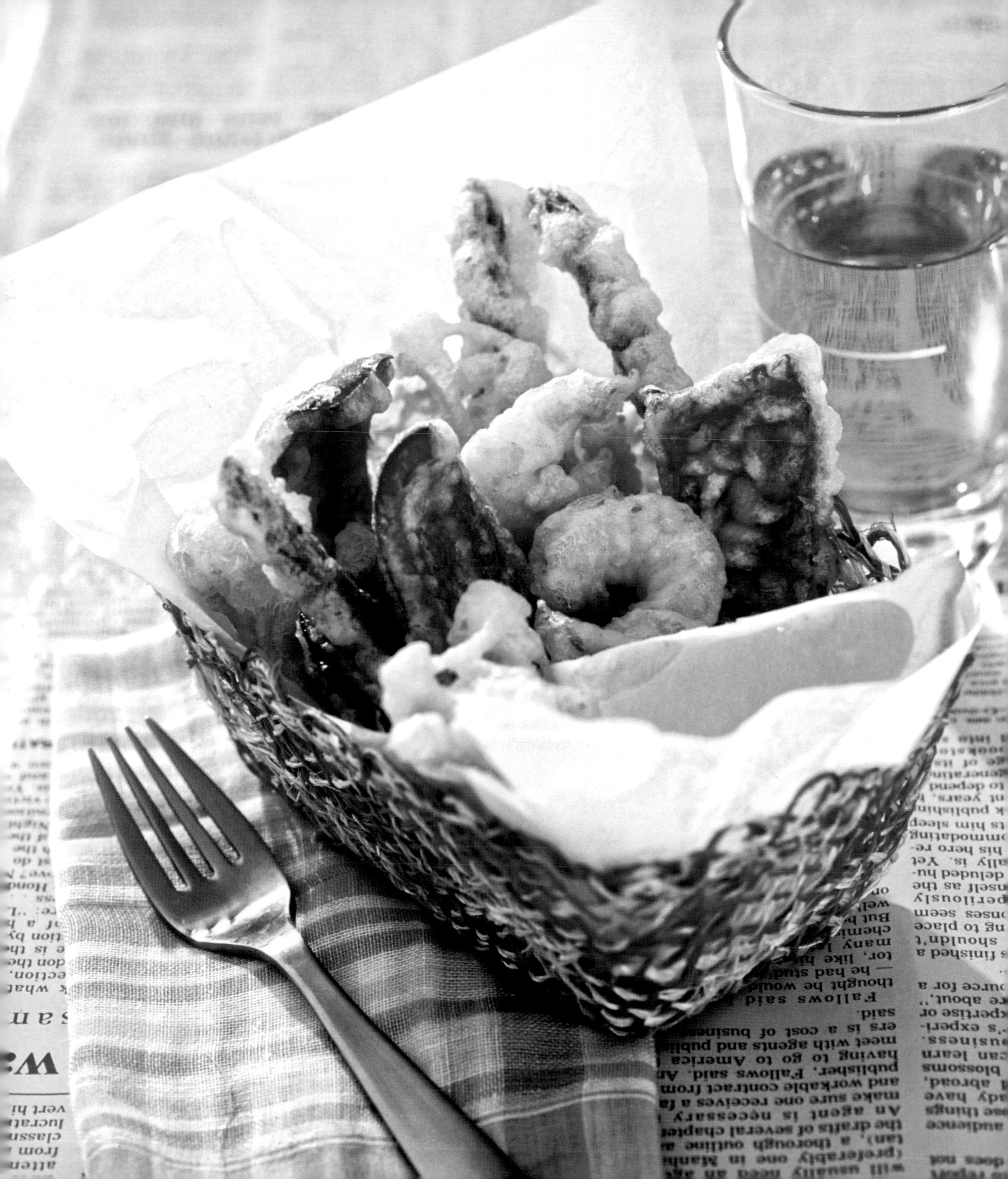

# POLENTA WITH BACON, SHRIMP AND CHIVES

The best polenta I have made was for this photo shoot. I combined two types of polenta (one coarse, the other medium-grain) and cooked the ground corn in home-made unsalted chicken stock, rather than just water, for a couple of hours, instead of the 45 minutes recommended on the packet. At the end, I whisked in a large chunk of top-quality butter, but didn't add grated parmesan cheese, because I was serving the polenta with shrimp. The texture was light and almost fluffy (as fluffy as polenta can be); it wasn't at all stodgy.

Shrimp and grits is a classic dish from the southern United States. Polenta is similar to grits - the main difference is the way the dried corn is processed. Polenta is a lot easier to find in Hong Kong so I use it instead of grits. Don't use instant polenta; it's not nearly as good as the type that needs to be simmered for a long time.

## INGREDIENTS

250 grams polenta (preferably a mix of coarsely ground and medium-grain polenta)
1.5 litres water or home-made unsalted chicken stock
Fine sea salt
120 grams unsalted butter
300 grams thick-cut bacon
12-16 large, fresh shrimp (with bodies about 8cm long), heads and shells removed, but leave the tail intact
12 (or more) chives (don't use Chinese chives)

## METHOD

1 Put the polenta and water (or chicken stock) in a medium-sized pan, season with salt and set the pan over a medium flame. Whisk constantly until the mixture comes to a boil. Lower the heat and simmer for five minutes, whisking constantly. Turn the heat as low as possible, then cover the pan with the lid.

2 Cook the polenta at a low simmer for at least one hour (although two is better), whisking frequently. The polenta will thicken and "spit" as it cooks, so take care not to get burned. If it seems too thick, whisk in more boiling water. Taste for seasonings and add salt, if needed. Add the butter and whisk until it melts completely.

3 Cut the bacon into 5mm pieces and cook in an unoiled skillet until it starts to brown. Drain the bacon on paper towels, but leave most of the bacon grease in the skillet. Dry the shrimp with paper towels. Heat the skillet over a medium flame and when it's hot, sear the shrimp on both sides and cook until done.

4 Ladle the polenta into shallow bowls. Arrange the shrimp on top, then scatter the bacon over the polenta. Use kitchen scissors to snip the chives into 1cm pieces over the polenta and serve.

Serves 6-8.

# STIR-FRIED RICE VERMICELLI WITH BELACAN, PORK BELLY AND SHRIMP

Belacan (fermented, dried shrimp paste) has an extremely strong smell that many find unpleasant, but it's essential to many Malaysian, Singaporean, Indonesian and Thai dishes. When cooked with other ingredients, the flavour softens and blends, adding richness. Use a Southeast Asian type of belacan (which comes as a hard block), not the Chinese fermented shrimp paste sold in a jar. You can add other ingredients such as bean sprouts (stir-fry them when cooking the onion, carrot and cloud ear mushrooms); scrambled egg that's been cooked into a thin flat pancake before being cut into strips; and blanched squid. Fresh lime, squeezed over the dish just before eating, is essential - the tartness perks up the flavour and makes the noodles feel less oily.

## INGREDIENTS

About 80ml cooking oil
150 grams rice vermicelli
20 grams cloud ear mushrooms
300 grams pork belly
15ml soy sauce
15ml rice wine
1/2 tsp granulated sugar
Fine sea salt and finely ground white pepper
1 heaped tsp cornstarch
1 medium-size onion
150 grams carrot
200 grams fresh shrimp, heads, tails and shells removed
5-10 grams belacan
1-2 red bird's-eye chillies
2 spring onions
1/2 a large red chilli
Fresh coriander sprigs
Lime wedges, for squeezing
Sambal or chilli oil

## METHOD

1 Soak the vermicelli in hot (not boiling) water for 30 minutes, then drain. Soak the cloud ear mushrooms in warm water until hydrated, then drain. Remove and discard the hard stem (if there is one) from the mushrooms and cut into strips about 2mm wide. Remove and discard the skin from the pork belly and cut it into pieces about 1cm wide and 3mm thick. Put the pork belly in a bowl, add the soy sauce, rice wine, sugar, cornstarch and a pinch each of salt and white pepper. Combine thoroughly and leave to marinate while preparing the other ingredients. Halve the onion and cut into thin slices. Julienne the carrot. Cut the shrimp into 1cm pieces. Wrap the belacan in a small piece of aluminium foil, put on an unoiled skillet and toast over a medium flame for a few minutes, turning the foil packet frequently so it doesn't burn. Cool the belacan. Slice the bird's-eye chillies into thin rounds. Cut the spring onions and red chilli into long, thin strips.

2 Heat a wok over a medium-high flame until very hot, then add about 30ml of cooking oil. When the oil is hot, add the pork belly and stir-fry until lightly browned. Add the shrimp and stir-fry until the pieces turn pink, then remove the pork and shrimp from the wok. Rinse the wok, put it over a medium-high flame and add 30ml of oil. Stir-fry the onion until slightly wilted, then add the carrot and mushrooms and stir-fry for about 30 seconds. Remove the vegetables from the wok. Heat 20ml of oil in the wok and, when hot, add the belacan. Use a spatula to break it up so no lumps remain. Add the bird's-eye chillies and stir-fry for 30 seconds. Add the rice vermicelli and mix thoroughly. Put the pork belly, shrimp, onion, carrot and mushrooms back into the wok, season lightly with salt and mix well. Add about 100ml of water, stir again, then cover with the lid, lower the heat and simmer, stirring occasionally, until the liquid is absorbed and the vermicelli is tender but not mushy (if necessary, add more water). Taste for seasonings, then stir in the spring onion, large red chilli and coriander. Serve with lime wedges and sambal or chilli oil.

Serves about 4.

# MUSSELS WITH POTATOES, PEPPERS AND ROUILLE

## INGREDIENTS

300 grams small potatoes (preferably no larger than 3cm long)
100 grams unsalted butter
1 large leek, white and pale green part only
4 garlic cloves, sliced
1 red bell pepper
1 yellow bell pepper
150ml dry white wine
1.2kg bouchot mussels
Fine sea salt and freshly ground black pepper

### FOR THE ROUILLE

1 potato (taken from the ones boiled for the mussels)
1 large egg yolk, at room temperature
2-4 garlic cloves, peeled and crushed to a paste
1/2 tsp piment d'Espelette or cayenne, or to taste
1/2 tsp saffron threads, roughly chopped, soaked in 15ml hot water, then cooled to lukewarm
250ml olive oil (or use 125ml olive oil and 125ml canola or grapeseed oil)
Fresh lemon juice, to taste
Thin baguette slices, toasted

## METHOD

**1** Scrub the potatoes but don't peel them. Put them in a pot and add enough cool, heavily salted water to cover them by about 2cm. Place the pot over a medium flame, bring to the boil, then lower the heat and simmer until they're just tender enough to be pierced with a knife; do not overcook them. Rinse them with cold running water. Set aside one potato (or two, if they're very small) for the rouille; cut the others in half.

**2** Make the rouille. Peel the potato and mash it to a smooth paste. Mix it with the egg yolk, crushed garlic, piment d'Espelette and a large pinch of salt. Whisking constantly, start adding the oil a drop or two at a time, making sure it's fully mixed in before adding more. Don't add the oil too quickly or the mixture will curdle; once you have a stable emulsion, start whisking in the oil in a very thin, steady stream. After adding about a quarter of the oil, whisk in some of the saffron threads and liquid. Continue to whisk in the oil, adding some saffron liquid intermittently. Taste the rouille and add salt and a little lemon juice, if needed.

**3** Trim off and discard the stem end of the leek. Slice the leek lengthwise into quarters then cut into 5mm pieces. Put the leek in a colander and rinse thoroughly under cold running water. Cut the bell peppers into 8mm strips.

**4** Put the butter in a wide pan large enough to fit the mussels (they'll expand as they open) and set it over a low flame. When the butter is half melted, add the leek and potatoes and season with salt and black pepper. Cook, stirring often, until the leek is soft. Add the garlic and bell peppers and cook over a medium flame until the peppers start to soften. Turn the heat to medium-high, add the white wine, bring to the boil and cook for about 90 seconds. Add the mussels, then cover the pan with the lid and simmer, shaking the pan frequently. Cook the mussels until they open (about three minutes).

**5** Toast the baguette slices, then spread some of the rouille over each piece. Ladle the mussels and the cooking liquid into bowls and serve with the rouille toast. If you like, add some rouille into the broth after eating the mussels, and drink it as a garlicky, spicy - and delicious - soup.

Serves 3-4.

# CHICKEN KARAAGE

I've become obsessed with bento – Japanese-style packed lunches. I haven't gone quite so far as to buy special moulds to shape hard-boiled eggs into kawaii anime characters, or cutters for making vegetables and sheets of nori look like flowers, nor have I always achieved the five colours (white, black/brown, red/orange, yellow and green) that a "balanced" bento box should have. And I certainly haven't been waking up an hour early to prepare my lunch ingredients. Most of the time, my bento box contains leftover Japanese rice (microwaved in the morning, to soften it) with furikake (flavoured rice sprinkles), meat and vegetables from a previous meal, home-made or purchased pickles, a little fruit and something sweet. I pack the food into a bamboo bento box and wrap it in a furoshiki cloth. Eating food out of a bento box is a lot more pleasurable than from a Tupperware container.

## INGREDIENTS

300 grams boneless chicken thighs
20ml soy sauce
10ml rice wine
2 garlic cloves, minced
1/2 tsp grated ginger
1/4 tsp finely ground white pepper
30 grams cornstarch
Cooking oil, for frying

## METHOD

**1** Cut the chicken into 2cm chunks, then mix with the soy sauce, rice wine, garlic, ginger and pepper. Marinate at room temperature for 30 minutes, or longer in the fridge.

**2** Pour cooking oil into a pan to a depth of about 3cm and heat to 180 degrees Celsius. Sprinkle the cornstarch over the chicken and mix thoroughly. Fry the chicken a few pieces at a time; do not crowd the pan. Drain on paper towels and cool completely before packing into a bento box.

Serves 2.

# THAI-STYLE CHICKEN WINGS

## INGREDIENTS

1kg chicken wings, wing tips removed
2 garlic cloves
2 red bird's-eye chillies, finely minced
The roots of several sprigs of fresh coriander, finely chopped
80ml bottled Thai fish sauce
20 grams granulated sugar
20ml fresh lime juice
A pinch of finely ground white pepper
Cooking oil, for frying
Optional: fresh chilli, lime wedges and coriander sprigs, to serve

## METHOD

1 Cut the wings to separate the drumette and middle joints.

2 Peel the garlic cloves, then use a pestle to pound them to a paste with the chillies and coriander root. Mix this paste with the fish sauce, sugar, lime juice and pepper. Add the wings and stir to combine. Cover with cling film and refrigerate for several hours, mixing occasionally.

3 Take the wings out of the fridge 30 minutes before cooking. Drain and pat them dry with paper towels. Heat cooking oil to a depth of about 3cm in a deep skillet. Add the wings a few at a time but do not overcrowd the pan. Fry the wings until they're medium brown and cooked through, then drain them on paper towels. If you like, garnish the wings with fresh chillies, lime wedges and coriander sprigs.

Serves 6 as part of a Thai meal.

# YELLOW EARTH CHICKEN

*Margaret Xu* opened her first restaurant, the tiny, one-table private kitchen Cuisine X, in Yuen Long in 2003. Foodies made the trek to the remote village house to taste Xu's dishes, which were created, whenever possible, with home-grown produce.

She still grows her own – or has farmers who do it for her – but she now serves her food at Yin Yang, which is in a grade-two heritage building on Ship Street, Wan Chai. As she's always done, Xu makes enough sauces and infusions from seasonal produce to last her throughout the year. One of her most famous dishes is yellow earth chicken, which she's been making since her Cuisine X days. The chicken, cooked in a terracotta oven made with two enormous plant pots, is rubbed with fruit wine (seasonal fruit infused in rice wine) and served with a sauce made of kencur ginger (sometimes called wild ginger), a type of galangal. Xu makes the sauce in sufficient quantities for when the rhizome is not available, although Chinese ginger spice powder works as a substitute.

## INGREDIENTS

FOR THE MARINADE AND SAUCE
**60ml extra-virgin olive oil**
**2 tbsp minced fresh kencur ginger, or 1 tbsp ginger spice powder (this is a spice blend sold at supermarkets)**
**About 20 small curry leaves, finely minced**
**2 tsp salt (add less salt if using ginger spice powder)**

FOR THE CHICKEN
**1 fresh chicken, about 1.2kg**
**About 1.5kg rock salt, divided**
**15ml fruit wine**
**Vegetable oil, as needed**

## METHOD

1 Make the marinade and sauce at least one day in advance so the flavours have time to blend. Thoroughly combine the kencur ginger (or ginger spice powder), curry leaf, salt and olive oil, then refrigerate overnight.

2 Put the fruit wine and half the marinade in the cavity of the chicken and rub it in to coat the interior thoroughly. Rub 1½ tbsp of rock salt over the skin of the chicken. Leave in the fridge for three or four hours.

3 Preheat the oven to 180 degrees Celsius. Very lightly dampen a sheet of parchment paper and use it to wrap the chicken securely. Very lightly spray (or brush) vegetable oil over the parchment (this helps to keep the chicken moist). Repeat with a second layer of lightly dampened parchment and sparingly spray or brush with vegetable oil.

4 Pour the remaining rock salt into a clean, dry wok and place over a medium flame. Stirring often, heat the rock salt until it's very hot (when it will start to darken). Spread about one-third of the salt in a Chinese sand pot large enough to hold the chicken. Put the parchment-wrapped chicken into the pot, taking care not to burn yourself on the hot salt. Pour the remaining salt over the chicken so it's completely covered.

5 Bake at 180 degrees for 45 minutes and carefully remove from the sand pot. Unwrap the chicken and put it on the serving dish. Xu serves the chicken whole, using scissors to cut it into pieces at the table. Serve with the remaining sauce.

Serves 6-8 as part of a Chinese meal.

Xu's original terracotta oven, which comprised two large, unpainted and unfinished pots, one upside-down on top of the other, used wood and charcoal to cook the food. At Yin Yang it's heated with gas. She likes to cook using the oven because it holds and conducts heat steadily and evenly, which makes it energy efficient. If you want one of these terracotta ovens in your backyard, look in gardening shops for the pots. Xu says heavy, dense pots are better than lightweight ones, which break easily. You'll need to saw the top off the inverted pot and attach a handle so it can be removed to allow food to be placed inside. The bottom pot will need an opening cut out for the fuel source. If that's too much work, Xu suggests cooking the chicken in a Chinese sand pot, which is what she uses to demonstrate the making of the dish. If using ginger spice powder as the dipping sauce (rather than fresh kencur), mix 1 tsp of hot oil to 1 tbsp of the powder.

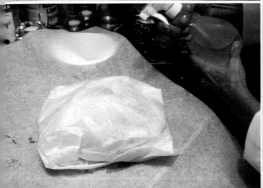
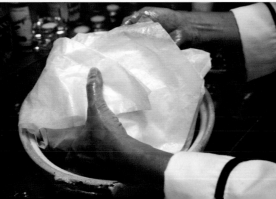

# TORTAS WITH SPICED FLANK STEAK, CRUSHED BLACK BEANS AND AVOCADO

## INGREDIENTS

One flank steak, about 600 grams
45ml olive oil
About 1/4 tsp cayenne pepper, or more to taste
About 1/4 tsp paprika, or more to taste
30ml fresh lime juice
1 can black beans
30 grams lard, rendered goose (or duck) fat or oil
2 large shallots, minced
4 large garlic cloves, minced and divided
1 or 2 bird's-eye chillies, minced (optional)

### TO SERVE

4-6 individual crusty rolls (about 12cm long)
150 grams Monterey Jack cheese, roughly grated
1/4 head iceberg lettuce, shredded
1 ripe avocado, peeled and sliced
1/2 white onion, thinly sliced into rings
Canned pickled jalapenos, drained
Fresh coriander sprigs
Fine sea salt and freshly ground black pepper, to taste

## METHOD

1 Sprinkle salt lightly but evenly over the steak and leave at room temperature for 30 minutes. Mix the olive oil, cayenne pepper, paprika, lime juice and two minced garlic cloves, and massage thoroughly into the meat. Marinate at room temperature for an hour, or longer in the fridge. If you refrigerate the steak, leave it at room temperature for 30 minutes before cooking it.

2 Drain the black beans, rinse them with cold water then drain again. Heat the lard, rendered fat or oil in a skillet. Add the shallots and the remaining two garlic cloves and cook over a low flame until soft. Stir in the bird's-eye chillies (if using) and cook until fragrant, then add the drained black beans. Cook the beans, stirring frequently, until they're hot, then crush them roughly with the back of a wooden spoon - they should be a little chunky. If the beans seem too dry, stir in a little water.

3 Preheat the oven to 180 degrees Celsius. Bake the rolls for about five minutes to crisp the crust. Cut the rolls in half parallel to the cutting board and scoop out a little of the interior to leave room for the filling.

4 Season the steak with black pepper. Heat a grill pan (preferably cast iron) until very hot and oil it lightly. Sear the flank steak for about three minutes on each side (for medium-rare). Leave for 10 minutes before carving against the grain into thin slices.

5 To make the tortas, spread the bottom of each roll with a spoonful of the warm black beans. Add some of the sliced steak, cheese, lettuce, avocado, onion, jalapenos and coriander, then sprinkle with salt and pepper. Put the top of the roll over the filling and press down to lightly compress the ingredients.

Serves 4-6.

# MAPO DOUFU

Restaurateur *Jean Paul Gauci* grew up in Marseilles and London. He trained as a chef at Michelin-starred restaurants such as Le Petit Nice in Marseilles and Lucas Carton (under Alain Senderens) in Paris, before coming to Hong Kong in 1990 after cooking stints in Japan and Taiwan. Soon after arriving here as a chef, Gauci began opening his own restaurants, serving such varied cuisines as Portuguese, Cuban, Vietnamese and Mediterranean.

In 2010 Gauci opened the Sichuan restaurant Bistro Jinli on a small, quiet street in Aberdeen, and hired as chef *Sze King Chun* (far right with Gauci), a native of Hubei. The food at Bistro Jinli is as spicy, pungent, oily and rich as Sichuan food should be. The chef cooks mapo doufu the way it was originally made – with minced beef rather than minced pork.

## INGREDIENTS

60 grams minced beef
A pinch of salt
1 tsp cornstarch
360 grams firm bean curd, cut into 2cm cubes
Cooking oil, as needed
2-3 tbsp chilli paste
1.5 tbsp chilli powder
1.5 tbsp Sichuan peppercorn powder
2.5 tbsp Sichuan fermented black beans, chopped
1 Chinese leek, sliced into 2.5cm pieces
About 300ml home-made chicken stock
1 tbsp light soy sauce
1 tbsp regular soy sauce
1 tbsp sesame oil
2 tbsp pepper oil
Cornstarch mixed with water, as needed
3 tbsp chilli oil
1 spring onion, minced

## METHOD

**1** Mix the beef with the salt and cornstarch and leave for about 30 minutes.

**2** Pour some water in a wok and heat over a high flame. When it's almost at the boil add the bean curd. Bring to the boil and cook for about a minute, then drain it.

**3** Heat the wok over a high flame and add enough oil to coat it lightly. Add the beef and stir-fry until it's about three-quarters cooked. Add the chilli paste and stir-fry until well combined.

Mix in the chilli powder, peppercorn powder and black beans and stir-fry until fragrant. Add the leek and chicken stock. Boil for about two minutes before gently mixing in the bean curd, light and regular soy sauces, sesame oil and pepper oil. Simmer for about a minute, then stir in some cornstarch/water mixture to thicken the sauce slightly. Stir in the chilli oil and simmer briefly. Transfer the ingredients to a deep bowl, sprinkle with spring onions and serve with steamed white rice.

Serves 6 as part of a Chinese meal.

# HONEYCOMB TRIPE WITH PARMESAN CHEESE

If possible, buy the tripe from the supermarket rather than a wet-market butcher because it will be easier to work with, having been thoroughly cleaned and blanched; if you buy it from the butcher, you'll have to wash it several times in heavily salted water, then it needs to be blanched a few times in boiling water.

This recipe is based on one in Marcella Hazan's *Essentials of Italian Cooking*. I ate a similar version at one of my favourite restaurants in Paris, Le Comptoir du Relais; the French version has potatoes and red bell peppers, which you can add. The tripe can be served on its own or with crusty bread, and it's delicious with polenta or pasta.

## INGREDIENTS

1kg honeycomb tripe, cleaned and blanched
45 grams unsalted butter, divided
60ml cooking oil
1/2 large onion, diced
1 celery stalk, diced
1 medium-sized carrot, diced
2 large garlic cloves, chopped
Dry chilli flakes, to taste
1 tsp fresh rosemary leaves, chopped
240ml red or dry white wine
250 grams diced Italian tinned tomatoes
250ml unsalted beef or chicken stock
Fine sea salt and freshly ground black pepper, to taste
75 grams freshly grated parmesan cheese, plus more for sprinkling at the table

## METHOD

Thaw the tripe, if it is frozen, then rinse it thoroughly and cut into 6cm x 1cm pieces. Heat the cooking oil and 15 grams of butter in a heavy-bottomed pot (preferably enamelled cast iron) over a low flame, then add the onion and cook until it turns pale golden. Stir in the celery, carrot, garlic, chilli flakes and rosemary and cook for one minute. Add the tripe and cook for five minutes, stirring occasionally, then stir in the wine. Bring to a simmer for 30 seconds, then stir in the tomatoes and meat stock. Bring back to a simmer, then lower the heat, cover the pan and cook slowly, stirring occasionally, until the tripe is tender (about two hours). If the tripe seems dry, add a little water; if it's watery, only partially cover the pan. When the tripe is tender and the sauce is at the right consistency, stir in 75 grams of parmesan cheese and the remaining butter. Serve immediately, with extra parmesan for sprinkling over the top.

Serves 4-6.

# OXTAIL BRAISED IN RED WINE

Have the butcher cut the oxtail into pieces between the joints. The larger pieces should be sawed in half through the bone.

## INGREDIENTS

30ml canola oil

2.5kg oxtail, cut into pieces

1 large carrot, diced

2 onions, diced

1 celery stalk, diced

100 grams tomato puree

1 litre dry red wine

80ml white vinegar

1 tsp sugar

4 thyme sprigs

1 bay leaf

1 tsp whole black peppercorns

3 garlic cloves, minced

225ml chicken stock

45ml fresh lemon juice

Fine sea salt and freshly ground black pepper, to taste

About 300 grams fresh pappardelle

## METHOD

**1** Preheat the oven to 150 degrees Celsius. Season the oxtail with salt and pepper. Heat a large, heavy pot, add the canola oil and when hot, brown the oxtail on all sides, then remove it from the pan.

**2** Add the carrot, onion and celery and cook until pale brown. Add the tomato puree and cook for two to three minutes. Stir in the wine, vinegar and sugar, bring to the boil, then simmer until the liquid is reduced by half. Add the thyme, bay leaf, peppercorns, garlic and browned oxtail. Stir in the stock and enough water to come halfway up the meat. Bring to a simmer, cover the pan with aluminium foil and place in the oven. Cook for 1 1/2 hours, then remove the foil and continue to cook until the oxtail is tender and the sauce has become more concentrated (about three hours in total). Turn the oxtail occasionally while cooking.

**3** Remove the oxtail from the pan. Spoon off the fat that has floated to the surface of the sauce. Strain the sauce through a colander into a bowl; discard the vegetables and herbs. Pour the sauce back into the pan; if necessary, simmer the sauce to reduce it until it lightly coats a spoon. Taste the sauce and correct the seasoning. Add the oxtail to the pan and keep warm over a low flame.

**4** Boil the pappardelle. When the pasta is al dente, drain it and add to the oxtail. Add the lemon juice and toss the pasta to coat it with the sauce.

Serves 4-6.

# MACCHIESI FAMILY SPAGHETTI AND POLPETTI

This is the family recipe of food stylist Rachael Macchiesi. Her mother, Patricia, visiting from Italy, kindly cooked the dish for the photoshoot.

## INGREDIENTS

FOR THE POLPETTI (MEATBALLS)

250 grams minced pork
250 grams minced beef
1 garlic clove, minced
1 large onion, roughly grated
1 1/2 tsp salt
1 tsp ground pepper
10 grams parsley, finely chopped
6 leaves fresh sage, finely chopped
2 egg yolks
40 grams breadcrumbs (preferably fresh, but dried is fine too), plus more for rolling the polpetti
60 grams finely grated parmesan, plus extra for sprinkling
45ml olive oil

FOR THE SAUCE

60ml olive oil
1 small onion, coarsely grated
2 garlic cloves, minced
240ml white wine
1 can (400 grams) diced tomatoes
15ml tomato paste
1 chicken stock cube
1/4 tsp sugar
600 grams spaghetti

## METHOD

1 To make the polpetti, combine the minced pork and beef with the garlic, onion, salt, pepper, parsley, sage, egg yolks, breadcrumbs and parmesan. Mix well with your hands. Use a tablespoon to scoop the mixture and shape into 30 to 40 balls. Coat in breadcrumbs. Heat the olive oil and pan-fry the meatballs in batches over a low flame for three to five minutes, browning them on all sides.

2 To make the sauce, heat the olive oil and cook the onion and garlic until soft. Add the white wine and let it simmer, then add the tomatoes, tomato paste, stock cube and sugar, and simmer for 45 minutes. Taste for seasoning and adjust if needed. Add the meatballs and simmer for 10 minutes.

3 Bring a pot of salted water to the boil. Cook the spaghetti until al dente and toss with the sauce and meatballs. Serve with extra parmesan cheese.

Serves 4-6.

# CHINESE ALMOND SOUP

Fook Lam Moon was a catering business before the Chui family established it as a restaurant in 1972. Often called "the tycoons' canteen", the restaurant has been in Lockhart Road, Wan Chai, since 1989, with branches in Tsim Sha Tsui as well as on the mainland and in Japan. A third-generation family member, *Daniel Chui* is a medical doctor but is perhaps better known as Fook Lam Moon's executive director. Although many of his wealthy clientele order delicacies such as sea cucumber and bird's nest, the restaurant also serves excellent versions of Cantonese classics, such as fried chicken, roast suckling pig, fried rice in lotus leaf and Chinese almond soup, which is requested in the evening by almost 50 per cent of Fook Lam Moon's diners. The recipe for that sweet soup calls for two types of Chinese almonds.

"The ingredients are very important," Dr Chui says, while watching executive chef *Lau Shing* (far right with Chui), who has worked at the restaurant for 40 years, make the dish. "You need Dragon King almonds with the skin on. Soak and peel them. Then for every four-to-six-person serving add four to six pieces of northern almonds, which are bitter; without them the soup is too rich and creamy."

Although the soup is not difficult to make, Dr Chui says, good ingredients are crucial, as is ample preparation time.

## INGREDIENTS

375 grams unpeeled Dragon King almonds
5 northern (bitter) almonds
37.5 grams granulated sugar

## METHOD

1 Bring a pan of water to the boil, add the Dragon King almonds, then bring to the boil again. Simmer the almonds for 10 minutes. Drain them, rinse with cold water and drain again. Peel the almonds and put them in a blender with the northern almonds, adding water to the 1.5-litre mark. Blend for five to six minutes. Moisten a large piece of fine-meshed, food-grade cheesecloth and squeeze out the almond milk.

2 Pour the almond milk into a saucepan, add the sugar and heat over a medium flame. Bring to a simmer, stirring constantly. Pour the soup into a tureen and skim off the bubbles with a ladle. Serve immediately.

Serves about 6.

---

Dragon King almonds, which are large and broad, are sometimes sold with the skin off, but Daniel Chui advises buying them intact and peeling them yourself because some sellers use chemicals to do the job.

Bak hung (northern almonds), also known as bitter almonds or apricot kernels, are available peeled at shops that sell ingredients for Chinese medicinal soups.

# SUMMER PUDDING

When I lived in San Francisco, I worked with Andrew, an English pastry chef who wanted to introduce traditional British desserts to the American public. They weren't very enthusiastic about things such as sherry trifle, fruitcake or Christmas pudding with brandy sauce, but summer pudding proved very popular.

Summer pudding is so easy to make that it almost doesn't need a recipe, but Andrew gave me several good tips. He said it should include some frozen fruit, which yields more liquid than the fresh variety and keeps the pudding moist. He also said that for larger puddings, a good guideline for the amount of fruit to use is the weight of the water needed to fill the mould: roughly the same weight of fruit will give you some leftover, but that can be used to garnish the pudding. Finally, the sugar-to-fruit ratio should be 1:10, although that can be adjusted according to the sweetness of the fruit.

To the fruit suggested below, you can add or substitute fresh cherries and/or purple plums. Don't use any pale stone fruits because the flesh discolours.

## INGREDIENTS

200 grams frozen raspberries
200 grams frozen blueberries
200 grams fresh strawberries
200 grams fresh currants, stems removed
200 grams fresh blackberries
About 100 grams granulated sugar
1/4 tsp fine sea salt
10-12 thin slices of sandwich bread, crusts removed
Mint leaves, to garnish
Double cream, to serve

## METHOD

1 Put the frozen berries in a bowl and let them thaw before mixing in the sugar and salt. Remove and discard the stems from the strawberries, then slice into 5mm-thick pieces. Add the strawberries, currants and blackberries to the bowl and mix everything together until the sugar is dissolved. Taste the fruit and adjust the sugar level, if needed. There should be quite a lot of liquid in the bowl.

2 Cut a round of bread to fit the bottom of a one-litre mould that's deeper than it is wide. Dip the round on both sides in the fruit liquid and place it in the mould. Slice the sandwich bread so it fits with each piece slightly overlapping in the mould, first dipping each slice on both sides in the fruit liquid before placing it in the mould. After the mould has been lined with bread, ladle the fruit and some of the liquid into the mould, completely filling it and pressing on it so it's firmly packed. Cut more bread to cover the fruit, again soaking it in liquid before laying it on top. Press firmly so the bread is flush with the top of the mould. Wrap the mould entirely and securely in cling film, in case any liquid is pressed out. Lay a plate directly on top of the mould so it slightly presses on the bread and filling. Refrigerate the pudding and the remaining fruit for at least six hours.

3 To serve, run a thin-bladed knife between the pudding and the mould, then carefully invert it onto a serving platter and lift away the mould. Spoon the remaining fruit and liquid over and around the pudding, then garnish with mint leaves before serving with double cream.

Serves about 8.

# BREAD PUDDING WITH CRÈME ANGLAISE AND WHISKY SAUCE

This is a super-rich dessert because it has a double dose of custard (in the bread pudding and the crème anglaise). The potent whisky sauce makes the pudding more sophisticated than the regular version, although it can be served without it. If you like, you can substitute brandy for the whisky.

For the pudding, use a soft, rich, eggy bread, such as brioche. If you have time, leave the sliced bread out to dry slightly. This will help it absorb the custard.

## INGREDIENTS

FOR THE CRÈME ANGLAISE

250ml cream
250ml milk
1/2 tsp fine sea salt
1 vanilla bean
110 grams granulated sugar, divided
4 large egg yolks

FOR THE BREAD PUDDING

Butter, for greasing the baking dish
5-8 slices of soft, eggy bread, cut about 8mm thick
2 large egg yolks
1 large egg
1/2 tsp fine sea salt
60 grams granulated sugar
1/8 tsp ground cinnamon
A little freshly grated nutmeg
250ml cream
100ml milk

FOR THE WHISKY SAUCE

200 grams unsalted butter
300 grams granulated sugar, divided
1 large egg
1/4 tsp fine sea salt
100ml whisky

## METHOD

1 Make the crème anglaise first so it has time to cool. Whisk the egg yolks and 70 grams of sugar in a bowl until thick. Set this aside. Place a fine-meshed sieve over a clean bowl and set this aside as well.

2 Pour the milk and cream into a saucepan, then add the salt and 40 grams of sugar. Cut the vanilla bean in half lengthwise and scrape out the seeds. Put the seeds and the pod into the pan and heat over a low-medium flame until the milk/cream simmers. Ladle about 100ml of this mixture into the bowl holding the yolk and sugar and whisk immediately. Repeat this twice - this slowly increases the temperature of the yolks so they don't curdle. Whisking constantly, pour the contents of the bowl into the pan. Place the pan over a low flame and start stirring the mixture with a wooden spoon. Stir slowly back and forth so the spoon comes in contact with the entire bottom of the pan. The crème anglaise is ready when it coats the back of the spoon and leaves a track when you draw your finger across it. Do not let the mixture simmer or it will curdle. Pour the sauce through the sieve into the clean bowl and let it cool to room temperature, stirring occasionally. Chill the mixture in the fridge.

3 Preheat the oven to 180 degrees Celsius. Liberally butter a ceramic baking dish that's about 3cm deep. Lay the bread slices in the dish, overlapping them slightly. Thoroughly whisk together the yolks, egg, salt, sugar, cinnamon and nutmeg until slightly foamy. Gradually stir in the cream and milk. Pour this mixture over the bread and leave it to stand for about 30 minutes, pressing down on the bread until it is saturated with the custard but not to the point where it's falling apart. Bake until the bread pudding puffs up slightly and the custard is set.

4 Make the whisky sauce while the pudding is baking. Melt the butter in a saucepan, add 200 grams of sugar and stir over a low flame until dissolved. In a bowl, whisk the egg with the salt and remaining sugar. Ladle about 100ml of the butter/sugar mixture into the egg and whisk until smooth. Repeat this once. Whisking constantly, pour the contents of the bowl into the pan, then place it over a low flame and stir constantly for several minutes. Whisk the whisky into the mixture. Stir constantly over a low flame for several minutes. Do not let it boil or it will separate.

Serve the bread pudding with the hot whisky sauce and chilled crème anglaise

Serves 4.

# FRIEN

These recipes are for the occasions when you don't mind making a little more effort than usual in the kitchen. Cooking for friends (and I hope that includes family) can be relaxing and fun and having others help prepare the food means nobody is overworked, which makes a meal all the more enjoyable.

DS

# FOCACCIA WITH PANCETTA, CARAMELISED ONIONS AND ROSEMARY

This dough is very moist - it can't be kneaded the way you would other types of bread doughs. It makes a deliciously chewy focaccia with large air holes. For plain focaccia, just leave off the toppings except for the rough-flaked sea salt.

## INGREDIENTS

450ml lukewarm water (35 degrees Celsius)

1 1/2 tsp active dry yeast

550 grams plain (all-purpose) flour or bread flour, more if needed

1 1/2 tsp fine sea salt

About 100ml extra virgin olive oil, divided

500 grams onions, thinly sliced

200 grams pancetta, sliced about 5mm thick

2-3 fresh rosemary sprigs

Rough-flaked sea salt (preferably Maldon), for sprinkling

## METHOD

1 Use some of the olive oil to grease a large bowl liberally. Pour the lukewarm water into another large bowl, sprinkle the yeast over it and let it dissolve. Add in the flour and fine sea salt and stir vigorously to mix the ingredients. The dough should be very moist and sticky but firm enough to form a loose ball that holds its shape briefly. If necessary, mix in a little more flour. Scoop the dough into the oiled bowl, drizzle more oil on top and rub it in with your hand so the dough is well coated. Cover the bowl with cling film and refrigerate for a few hours or overnight.

2 Heat about 30ml of olive oil in a skillet, add the sliced onion and cook over a low flame, stirring frequently, until very soft and sweet - about 30 to 45 minutes. Cool to room temperature. Cut the pancetta into thick strips about 2cm long. Heat 10ml of olive oil in a skillet and cook the pancetta until soft but not browned, then cool to room temperature.

3 Let the dough come to room temperature before baking it. Preheat the oven to 240 degrees. Liberally oil one or two baking pans - I use two pans (about 20cm x 28cm) but you can also make one large free-form loaf. Use an oiled hand to transfer the dough to the pan(s). Press and stretch the dough until it's about 1cm thick. Use your fingertips to press deep indentations all over the dough, all the way down to the baking pan. Liberally oil the surface than spread the onions and pancetta evenly on top. Break the rosemary sprigs into small pieces and scatter over the surface, then sprinkle with coarse sea salt. Put the dough in the oven (there's no need to let the dough rise first) and immediately reduce the heat to 220 degrees and bake for 15 minutes. Turn the heat to 200 degrees and bake until the focaccia is fragrant, golden brown and firm to the touch. If the onions at the edge of the focaccia start to burn, use aluminium foil strips to cover them. Cool for 30 minutes before slicing.

Serves at least 8.

# CHICKPEAS WITH KABOCHA , CURRY AND YOGURT

I used to make this dish with just chickpeas, but I love the sweetness added by the kabocha. This recipe makes a lot, so the amounts can be halved.

## INGREDIENTS

600 grams kabocha
45ml olive oil
2 cans (about 400 grams each) chickpeas
1 1/2 tbsp curry powder, or to taste
2 tsp finely minced fresh ginger, or to taste
4 large shallots, peeled and minced
50ml fresh lime juice, or to taste
300 grams whole milk yogurt
A few drops each of Tabasco and
Worcestershire sauce
Finely minced fresh chillies, to taste
A large handful of fresh coriander, chopped
Fine sea salt and freshly ground black pepper,
to taste

TO SERVE
Harissa or chilli sauce

## METHOD

1 Preheat the oven to 200 degrees Celsius. Cut the kabocha into thick wedges and scrape out the seeds, then use a sharp heavy knife to remove the rind. Cut the flesh into 1cm pieces, drizzle with olive oil and sprinkle lightly with salt and pepper. Place the kabocha in one layer on a baking dish and roast, stirring occasionally, until it's firm-tender and lightly charred in spots. Allow to cool.

2 Drain the chickpeas, rinse them under cold running water and drain again. Dry thoroughly in a clean dish towel.

3 Cook the curry powder in a dry, unoiled skillet over a medium flame, stirring constantly until it darkens and smells toasted and fragrant; do not let it burn. Transfer the curry powder to a dish and let it cool. Mix the curry powder with the ginger, shallots, lime juice, yogurt, Tabasco, Worcestershire sauce and salt and pepper to taste. Combine this with the chickpeas, then gently mix in the kabocha, chillies and coriander. Taste for seasonings and adjust if necessary. Leave for an hour at room temperature so the flavours have time to blend. Add harissa or chilli sauce to taste.

Serves 8-10.

# GRILLED QUAILS WITH BABY SPINACH, ARUGULA, BEETROOT AND MUSTARD DRESSING

I usually dislike green salads because they leave me hungry but this one is substantial enough to serve as a meal. The recipe is by Vivian Herijanto.

## INGREDIENTS

4 quails, about 150 grams each, thawed, if frozen
80 grams arugula
60 grams baby spinach
4 small to medium beetroots, boiled until tender then peeled
2 tsp white vinegar
Cooking oil, for the grill
Fine sea salt, rough-flaked sea salt and freshly ground black pepper

FOR THE MUSTARD DRESSING
2 large egg yolks, at room temperature
1 garlic clove, minced
15 grams Dijon mustard
15 grams whole-grain mustard
360ml canola oil
About 20ml fresh lemon juice
15ml balsamic vinegar

## METHOD

1 Make the dressing by whisking the egg yolks in a bowl, then mixing in the garlic and mustards. Slowly whisk in the oil, a little at a time, to create an emulsion, letting each addition absorb fully before adding more. After all the oil has been incorporated, add the lemon juice and balsamic vinegar then add salt and pepper to taste. Add a little more lemon juice if needed to balance the flavours.

2 Bone the quails. Place each bird, breast-side down, on a cutting board. Use kitchen shears to cut along one side of the backbone, from the tail to the neck. Cut along the other side of the backbone to remove it. Open the quail and lay it skin-side up, then press firmly with your hand to flatten it. Remove the bones: most can be pulled out with your fingers; the others (such as the breast bone) can be removed by scraping away the flesh with a knife to loosen the bone. Scrape away the flesh at the thigh bone and cut it off where it attaches to the drumstick. Cut off the wing tip. When finished, the only bones will be in the drumstick and two joints of the wing. Sprinkle salt and pepper on both sides of each bird. Heat a cast-iron grill pan until it's very hot and brush with oil. Grill the quails for about three minutes on each side or until cooked to your liking.

3 Toss the arugula and spinach with 60ml of the dressing, lightly coating the leaves. Thinly slice the beets, toss with the white vinegar and arrange the slices around four plates. Place a mound of the greens on each plate, top with a quail (halved) and sprinkle with rough-flaked sea salt. Drizzle more of the dressing around the plate and serve.

Serves 4.

# SLICED PORK WITH CHILLI AND GARLIC SAUCE

*Chan Fugui* is the Sichuan executive chef of He Jiang restaurant at the Cosmopolitan Hotel in Wan Chai. A native Sichuanese, he worked for 10 years in Shanghai, a period that included a stint at Ye Shanghai by Elite Concepts, before moving to the restaurant group's He Jiang in 2012.

The sliced pork belly with garlic and chilli sauce that chef Chan makes is a classic Sichuan dish. He Jiang's version is beautifully presented and full of flavour.

The recipe for the flavoured soy sauce will give you much more than needed for this dish. The remainder can be filtered, decanted into a bottle and refrigerated.

## INGREDIENTS

500 grams well-layered, skin-on pork belly
15 grams ginger slices
15 grams spring onions

FOR THE FLAVOURED SOY SAUCE
250ml light soy sauce
60ml regular soy sauce
250 grams sugar
20 grams star anise
20 grams bay leaf
20 grams cinnamon stick

TO SERVE
250 grams long, thin cucumber
50ml chilli oil
50ml flavoured soy sauce
20 grams garlic, mashed
2 tsp sesame seeds
10 grams spring onions, minced

## METHOD

1 Put the pork belly, ginger and spring onions in a saucepan, cover with cool water and bring to a boil over a medium flame. Lower the heat so the water is at a bare simmer, partially cover with a lid and cook for 45 minutes. Drain the meat and cool it at room temperature, then wrap it in cling film and chill in the fridge for an hour. Remove from the fridge, place the pork belly on a flat surface, then put a pan on top with weights on it to flatten the meat slightly to an even thickness. Leave at room temperature for two hours. Trim the meat into an even block.

2 To make the flavoured soy sauce, put all the ingredients into a saucepan and bring to the boil. Lower the heat and simmer for one hour, then cool and strain.

3 Peel the cucumber and cut into lengths that are the same height as the piece of pork. Remove the seeds and cut the cucumber into pieces about 6mm thick. After slicing the meat very thinly (about 2mm), lay one piece of cucumber on each slice of pork belly and roll it tightly. Place the spirals upright on a serving plate and top each piece with a little mashed garlic. Drizzle chilli oil and soy sauce on top and scatter with sesame seeds and spring onions before serving.

Serves about 10 as part of a Chinese meal.

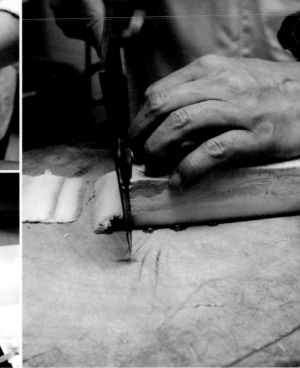

# CHERRY TOMATO AND RICOTTA TART WITH WHOLE-WHEAT AND OLIVE-OIL CRUST

This tart dough is based on one that I found on the Chocolate & Zucchini blog. I've changed the proportions of whole wheat to plain flour to make the crust more tender.

## INGREDIENTS

### FOR THE PASTRY

75 grams whole-wheat flour
175 grams plain (all-purpose) flour, plus extra for rolling
1/2 tsp fine sea salt
1 tsp dried thyme leaves, roughly crumbled
60ml extra-virgin olive oil
100ml iced water

### FOR THE FILLING

350 grams large cherry tomatoes
10ml olive oil
1 garlic clove, minced
5 grams parmesan cheese
1 thyme sprig, leaves only

### FOR THE RICOTTA CUSTARD

3 large eggs
250 grams ricotta
100ml cream
Fine sea salt and freshly ground black pepper

## METHOD

1 In a bowl, thoroughly combine the whole-wheat flour, plain flour, salt and thyme leaves. Drizzle the olive oil over the ingredients and use a fork to mix it in. Add the iced water and mix until the dough forms a rough mass. The dough should be soft but not sticky; if it is sticky, mix in a little more flour. Knead it briefly then wrap in cling film and refrigerate for at least an hour. On a lightly floured work surface, roll out the dough until it's very thin (about 2mm) and fit it into a tart pan with a removable bottom (use a rectangular tin that's about 33cm x 15cm and about 2cm deep, or a 23-25cm round tin). Ease the dough into the contours of the pan - do not stretch it. Trim off the dough so it's flush with the edges and refrigerate for about 30 minutes. Use a fork to poke holes at 1.5cm intervals over the bottom of the dough so it doesn't puff up when it bakes. Preheat the oven to 200 degrees Celsius. Put the tart pan in the oven and bake for 10 minutes, then turn the heat to 180 degrees and bake until it's fragrant and pale golden, about 10 more minutes. Remove from the oven and cool to room temperature. Increase the oven temperature to 200 degrees.

2 Cut the tomatoes in half and put them in a pan that fits them in one layer. Drizzle with the olive oil and add the parmesan, thyme leaves and minced garlic. Mix to coat the tomatoes evenly and arrange the pieces cut-side up in the pan. Bake at 200 degrees for about 20 minutes, or until slightly shrivelled but not collapsed. Cool for about 10 minutes. Leave the oven on.

3 In a food processor, mix the eggs with the ricotta and cream until smooth. Season with salt and pepper.

4 Put the tart shell (still in the pan) on a baking sheet and fill it halfway with the egg/ricotta mixture. Arrange the tomatoes close together in the shell and, if necessary, add more custard so it's filled close to the brim. Bake for 10 minutes, lower the heat to 180 degrees and continue baking until the custard is set (about 15 more minutes). Cool for at least 15 minutes before slicing. If there are any tomatoes and custard leftover, bake them together in a buttered ramekin.

Serves 6-8.

# KIMCHI PANCAKES

This batter is quite versatile - you can mix in chopped vegetables, seafood and meat. I like the slight chewiness that comes from a combination of potato starch (sometimes called potato flour) and regular flour. The recipe is based on one in *Growing Up in a Korean Kitchen* by Hi Soo Shin Hepinstall. Restaurants make large pancakes and cut them into pieces but I prefer to make smaller, individual ones.

## INGREDIENTS

FOR THE PANCAKES
**150 grams cabbage kimchi**
**120 grams minced pork**
**1 large egg**
**70 grams potato starch/flour**
**70 grams plain (all-purpose) flour**
**240ml iced water**
**Fine sea salt and ground white pepper**
**4-6 spring onions, cut into 3cm lengths**
**Red and green large, mild Thai chillies, sliced about 3mm thick**
**Oil, for pan frying**

FOR THE VINEGAR SOY SAUCE
**30ml soy sauce**
**30ml Korean or Japanese rice wine**
**30ml rice vinegar**
**15ml sesame oil**
**1 tsp lightly toasted white sesame seeds**
**A pinch of Korean chilli powder (optional)**

## METHOD

1 Put the kimchi in a colander and press gently with paper towels to extract some of the excess liquid - the kimchi shouldn't be too dry or dripping wet. Finely chop the kimchi and put it into a bowl. Add the pork, egg, potato and plain flours, water and salt and pepper to taste. Mix gently and refrigerate for about an hour (this lets the batter thicken as the starches absorb the liquid). Mix the sauce ingredients and transfer to a small serving bowl.

2 Heat a skillet over a medium flame and rub it lightly with oil. When it is hot, arrange two or three pieces each of the spring onion and chilli in a tight pattern in the skillet. Stir the batter and ladle in enough of it to cover the spring onion and chilli and to form a pancake about 6cm in diameter. Leave the pancake to cook undisturbed until the surface edges look as if they're drying out, then flip it over and cook the other side. Transfer to a baking sheet lined with paper towels and cook the remaining batter. Serve with the dipping sauce.

Serves 6-8 as part of a Korean meal.

# OCTOPUS CARPACCIO WITH OLIVE OIL, STICKY BALSAMIC AND SWEET PAPRIKA

The venue that had long been home to Lan Kwai Fong institution Post 97 underwent a radical change in January 2012. Gone were the bar snacks and dishes suited to soaking up alcohol late at night or early in the morning. Gone, too, was the dark interior. Reincarnated as Il Posto 97, the space has been modernised and now offers a menu by the Epicurean Group's executive chef, *Brian Moore*, who has been with the company since 2007. Moore introduced a raw bar and dishes such as house-made scallop and prawn tortellini with crustacean consomme, Sicilian-style bouillabaisse and twice-roasted duckling with Tuscan black cabbage.

Moore, who hails from Melbourne, learned how to handle octopus from a Japanese chef who was working in Australia. He pounds the octopus tentacles with Japanese daikon, which releases a tenderising enzyme that also assists in gelatinisation when the meat cooks. The technique doesn't work with the more commonly available Chinese white radish.

Moore buys octopus tentacles that have been "tumbled" (put in a machine that agitates the tough meat to soften it). If the octopus you buy hasn't been tumbled, pound it longer with the daikon. To cook the octopus you need a large steamer at least 25cm in diameter.

## INGREDIENTS

FOR THE REDUCED BALSAMIC:

**250ml regular Italian balsamic vinegar**
**80 grams granulated sugar**
**40 grams honey**

FOR THE OCTOPUS AND TO FINISH THE DISH

**1 Japanese daikon**
**500 grams fresh octopus tentacles**
**25 grams Maldon salt**
**70ml extra-virgin olive oil (chose one that's not too bitter)**
**Reduced balsamic, as needed**
**Sweet paprika, as needed**

## METHOD

1 Put the balsamic and sugar in a stainless steel pot and stir to dissolve the sugar. Place over a low-medium flame; do not cook it too quickly or the glaze will be bitter. Cook for 10-15 minutes, or until it reduces by at least three-quarters and has the consistency of runny honey (it will thicken as it cools). Remove from the heat and cool to room temperature, then stir in the honey. Transfer to a squeeze bottle. It will keep in the fridge for at least a month.

2 Rinse the octopus tentacles and dry them with paper towels. Put the tentacles in a large stainless steel bowl and sprinkle with the salt. Peel the daikon, rinse it and pat dry. Cut off one end of the daikon, then, holding it as if it were a pestle, pound the tentacles, turning them and mixing them occasionally. Pound for about five minutes (or longer) until the tentacles begin to release a slightly foamy residue. Do not rinse the tentacles, but use paper towels to wipe off the excess foam.

3 Place a sushi mat, smooth-side up, on the work surface. Lay the tentacles across the mat, overlapping them and piling them on top of each other as needed to form a cylinder that's as evenly thick as possible. Roll the sushi mat around the tentacles so they are firmly and securely encased. Use butcher string to tie the mat tightly at both ends and in the middle. Tightly roll the entire cylinder in two layers of cling film, then in two layers of aluminium foil, twisting the ends to form a tight seal.

Heat water in a steamer to a rapid boil. Steam the octopus parcel for 30 minutes, then remove it from the steamer and immediately put it in the freezer. Chill it for two to three hours, or until it reaches 1 degree Celsius. Take the octopus from the freezer and refrigerate it for 12 hours.

4 Remove the foil, plastic wrap and sushi mat from the octopus. Pat it dry, wiping away any excess jelly on its exterior. Wrap it tightly in cling film (this helps hold the tentacles in place when slicing it). Use a very sharp knife to trim the uneven ends, then slice the octopus to a thickness of 3mm. Arrange the slices evenly on a plate, using eight to 10 pieces per portion. Remove the plastic wrapping from the octopus slices.

5 Drizzle extra-virgin olive oil over the octopus and squeeze dots of the balsamic reduction onto the plate. Dust sweet paprika over the portions and serve.

Serves 8-10.

Moore says the object of putting the steamed octopus in the freezer is to cool it down as rapidly as possible to 1 degree Celsius, but emphasises that you should not freeze it. Clear as much space as possible in your freezer before cooking the octopus.

# GRILLED BAMBOO CLAMS WITH GARLIC, BUTTER AND PARSLEY

Buy the clams on the day you plan to cook them. The vendor will usually offer to clean them; accept, with alacrity. If cleaning them yourself, trim off the stomach and any other dark spots.

## INGREDIENTS

12-16 bamboo clams, about 10cm long, cleaned
and trimmed
1-2 large garlic cloves, finely minced
60 grams unsalted butter, melted
Fresh parsley, minced
Lemon or lime wedges

## METHOD

Divide the garlic among the clams, rubbing it into the meat. Liberally brush the clams with butter and place on a baking tray. Cook under a grill on high heat for about three minutes, or until sizzling. Brush with more butter, scatter with parsley and serve with lemon or lime wedges.

Serves 6-8 as a starter.

# SAUTÉED SLICED ABALONE WITH ONION AND WILD MUSHROOMS

*Ken Yu* lends a modern touch to the Chinese dishes served at Cuisine Cuisine in the Mira Hong Kong Hotel, Tsim Sha Tsui (another branch of the restaurant is in the IFC, Central). Not only is the Chinese executive chef's food delicious, it's also presented creatively and attractively. His dish of South African abalone stir-fried with mushrooms, for example, is served in what looks at first to be the usual fried potato or taro "nest" that other restaurants use. Closer examination shows that Yu's nest is made from bamboo pith, the lacy-looking fungus that grows over the tips of bamboo. Yu soaks it, squeezes out the water, dusts it in flour, then shapes it around a soup bowl as he fries it. The home cook might find it easier to try a simpler presentation.

## INGREDIENTS

2 fresh South African abalone, with shells about 8cm in length
Fine sea salt, as needed
80 grams ganoderma mushroom, sliced
80 grams straw mushrooms, halved
100 grams onion, sliced to a thickness of about 5mm 50 grams mild red chillies, cut into diamond shapes
2-3 garlic cloves, sliced
100 grams spring onions, cut into 4cm-5cm lengths
A little granulated sugar
A little ginger spice powder (this is a spice blend sold at supermarkets), or to taste
About 5 grams oyster sauce, or to taste
Cornstarch mixed with water, as needed
Oil, as needed

## METHOD

1 Sprinkle salt thoroughly over the exposed surface of the abalone and use a clean toothbrush to scrub it thoroughly (this rids it of the slime). Rinse it well under cool running water. Detach the abalone from the shell, leaving behind the liver. Pull out and discard the intestines and other internal organs from the abalone, then rinse it again.

2 Lay the abalone on a cutting board and hold it firmly. Use a very sharp, slender knife to slice the abalone into thin pieces parallel to the cutting board.

3 Heat oil to a depth of about 8cm in a wok. When the oil is hot add both types of mushroom and fry them briefly. Drain them and dip in boiling water mixed with salt and sugar to rinse off the oil. Drain again. Use the same oil to fry the onions quickly, then drain them.

4 Put the abalone slices in a flat metal strainer. Mix a ladleful of the hot oil with an equal amount of room-temperature oil to cool it down. Pour this over the abalone slices, then drain. Pour the oil from the wok but do not wash it. Heat the wok again, add the onions and mushrooms and stir-fry briefly. Add the chillies, garlic and spring onions and mix. Stir in the abalone and season to taste with salt, sugar, ginger spice powder and oyster sauce. Stir-fry briefly, then mix in a little cornstarch dissolved in water, using just enough that the sauce lightly coats the ingredients. Transfer to a plate and serve.

Serves 4-6 as part of a Chinese meal.

---

This seems like a lot of oil for a stir-fried dish but it can be filtered and re-used.

Frying the mushrooms in the hot oil, then blanching them in boiling water mixed with salt and sugar gives them more flavour.

Once you start stir-frying, keep the flame under the wok at a steady heat and don't over-cook the ingredients.

Chef Yu likes the Peacock abalone because he says that variety is best for slicing and stir-frying. It is available in large wet markets, but is quite expensive compared to other types of fresh abalone.

# SEARED TUNA WITH CORN, AVOCADO SALSA AND IKURA

This idea came from a photograph posted on Facebook by a friend. Her husband, who's a chef, had cooked a similar dish for dinner. It's fast, easy and delicious, and everything but the tuna can be prepared in advance. Don't overcook the tuna steak or it will be dry and heavy - sear it for no more than a minute in total.

## INGREDIENTS

10ml cooking oil
2-3 ears of corn, husks and silk removed
2 avocados
150 grams cherry tomatoes, diced
1 shallot, minced
Juice of one lime, or to taste
1-2 red bird's-eye chillies, minced
Fresh coriander leaves
2 tuna fillets, about 250 grams each and at least 2cm thick
About 15ml olive oil
About 30 grams ikura (salmon roe)
Fine sea salt and freshly ground black pepper

## METHOD

1 Cut each ear of corn in half. Stand each piece on the flat side and use a sharp knife to cut the kernels from the cob. Heat the cooking oil in a wok and when it's very hot, add the corn and a light sprinkling of salt. Stir-fry over a high flame until some of the kernels start to brown (some will pop, too), then remove from the wok and let them cool.

2 Cut the avocados in half and remove the pit. Use a sharp paring knife to cut the avocado into cubes while it's still in the shell (take care not to cut through the shell into your hand). Use a large spoon to scoop the avocado from the shell into a bowl. Add the tomatoes and shallot and season to taste with lime juice, minced chillies and salt and pepper. (The mixture will keep for a couple of hours in the fridge before the avocado turns brown.) Just before serving, mix in the coriander.

3 Thoroughly coat the tuna fillets with olive oil. Heat a seasoned cast-iron pan over a high flame until it starts to smoke. Sear the tuna steaks for 30 seconds, then flip and sear the other side. Remove from the heat and sprinkle lightly with salt.

4 To serve this as a main course, divide the corn between two plates and top each portion with a piece of tuna sliced to a thickness of about 8mm. Spoon the avocado salsa on top and add the ikura. To serve this as an appetiser, cut the tuna into 1cm cubes. Put the corn into four to six clear bowls, then add the tuna cubes and a large dollop of the avocado salsa. Top with the ikura and serve immediately.

Serves 2 as a main course, 4-6 as a starter.

# NASI LEMAK WITH SPICY PRAWNS

This recipe was developed by Vivian Herijanto. The sambal goreng keeps in the fridge for a few weeks - it should be made at least a few days before you cook the rest of the dish so the flavours have time to develop. The sambal is stirred into the prawns at the last minute. The ikan bilis can be made a couple of days in advance and stored in an air-tight container.

## INGREDIENTS

### FOR THE SAMBAL GORENG
6 garlic cloves, peeled
300 grams shallots, peeled
4 candlenuts (sold at shops specialising in Indonesian, Malaysian or Singaporean ingredients)
10-15 dried chillies, roughly chopped
30 grams tamarind pulp
200ml warm water
90ml vegetable oil
30 grams tomato paste
10-15 grams sugar
Fine sea salt, to taste

### FOR THE IKAN BILIS
Oil, for frying
40 grams dried baby anchovies
80 grams raw red-skinned peanuts
30 grams red finger chillies
200 grams shallots, peeled
4 garlic cloves, peeled
1 tsp belacan (shrimp paste)
15 grams tamarind pulp
60ml water
10-15 grams sugar
15 grams tomato paste
Fine sea salt, to taste

### FOR THE RICE
300 grams jasmine rice
400ml coconut milk (canned is fine)
100ml water
2 pandan leaves, tied into a knot
About 2 tsp fine sea salt

### TO SERVE
4 large eggs, at room temperature
About 500 grams fresh prawns, with bodies about 6cm in length
1 cucumber, peeled, halved and cut on the diagonal into 5mm thick slices
Fresh banana leaves, cut into sheets about 30cm square (optional)

## METHOD

1 Finely grind the garlic, shallots, candlenuts and chillies in a mortar or food processor. The mixture should be a moist paste; if necessary, add a little water. Stir 200ml of warm water into the tamarind pulp and break it up with a spoon to dissolve it as much as possible. Strain the liquid, pressing the pulp through the sieve to extract as much flavour as possible. Set the liquid aside.

2 Heat the oil in a wok or skillet set over a low flame. When the oil is very hot, add the garlic/shallot/candlenut/chilli paste and stir constantly until it's thick, fragrant and shiny. Stir in the tomato paste, tamarind liquid, sugar and about two teaspoons of salt. Stir well, taste the mixture and adjust the seasonings if needed. Continue cooking until thick, then transfer to a bowl or jar. When the sambal is cool, cover the bowl or jar and refrigerate. The oil that floats to the surface should be stirred into the mixture before use.

3 Soak the anchovies in warm water until they're pliable. Drain them, then pull the heads straight off the bodies - if you do it with the right motion, this should also pull out their innards. Lay the anchovy bodies on a layer of paper towels and let them air-dry.

4 Pour oil to a depth of about 4cm in a wok and heat it over a medium-low flame until ripples appear on the surface. Add the peanuts and stir-fry constantly until golden. Remove them from the oil with a slotted spoon, drain on paper towels and sprinkle lightly with salt. Turn the flame to low and fry the anchovies, stirring constantly, until they're golden brown and crisp through. Remove the anchovies from the oil, drain on paper towels and mix them with the peanuts.

5 Grind the finger chillies with the shallots, garlic and belacan to a paste in a mortar or food processor. Mix the tamarind pulp with the water, stir to dissolve, then strain the liquid through a sieve. Heat 60ml of fresh oil in a clean wok over a medium-high flame and when it's hot, add the spice paste and fry, stirring constantly, until it's thick and fragrant. Add the tamarind liquid, sugar, tomato paste and salt to taste and stir to blend well. Bring the sauce to a simmer, then remove from the heat. Mix some of the sauce with the anchovies and peanuts to lightly coat them. Put the remaining sauce into a bowl.

6 Rinse the rice in several changes of water until it runs clear. Drain well, put the rice in a rice cooker and stir in the

coconut milk, water and pandan leaves. Leave for 30 minutes, then stir in the salt and cook the rice until tender.

**7** Put the eggs in a pan just large enough to fit them in one layer. Add enough water to cover the eggs by about 1cm. Place the pan over a medium flame, bring to the boil and remove from the heat. Cover the pan with the lid and leave for 10 to 12 minutes. Drain the eggs and put them in a bowl of iced water. When the eggs are completely cool, peel them and cut in halves or quarters.

**8** Peel the prawns but leave the heads intact, if desired. Slit the prawns down the back and remove the black vein. Heat about 200 grams of the sambal goreng in a skillet, then add the prawns and simmer until they're pink, curling and cooked through. The prawns should be liberally coated with the sambal; if necessary, add more to the pan.

To serve, scoop some of the rice onto the banana leaves. Add some prawns, spiced ikan bilis, sliced cucumber and an egg to each portion. Serve the remaining sauce (used to coat the ikan bilis) and sambal on the side.

Serves 4.

# ANGEL HAIR PASTA WITH UNI, TOMATOES AND GARLIC CHIPS

*Tony Cheng* was a banker before deciding he'd rather be a chef. After working with friend and mentor Roland Schuller at the Austrian chef's restaurant Aspasia, Cheng moved to Rome to work as an apprentice at All'Oro restaurant. When Cheng returned to Hong Kong, he and a business partner opened The Drawing Room in Causeway Bay with Schuller in the team. Cheng's restaurant group, Drawing Room Concepts, expanded to include a chain of Hainan chicken rice restaurants called Hainan Shaoye; Le Salon Restaurant et Croissanterie, which specialises in croissants; and Ammo, at the Asia Society Hong Kong Center.

On the menu at Ammo is the popular angel hair with uni, tomatoes and garlic chips – one of the few dishes with uni as delicious cooked as it is raw.

Cheng uses an interesting technique to make the pasta inherently flavourful: he dips it in boiling water just long enough for it to soften, then cooks it in scampi stock.

This recipe is for one portion; increase proportionately to serve more.

## INGREDIENTS

FOR THE SCAMPI STOCK

**50ml olive oil**
**1kg scampi**
**150 grams leeks, white part only, cut into brunoise, rinsed thoroughly and drained**
**150 grams large fennel bulb, rinsed and cut into brunoise**
**150 grams carrots, rinsed and cut into brunoise**
**150 grams celery, rinsed and cut into brunoise**
**5 garlic cloves, sliced**
**100 grams cherry tomatoes, halved**
**1 tbsp tomato paste**
**130ml brandy or cognac**
**A bouquet garni (1 bay leaf, 1 thyme sprig and 1 oregano sprig, tied together with string)**

FOR THE GARLIC OIL AND CHIPS

**40 grams garlic, thinly sliced**
**200ml olive oil**

FOR THE PASTA AND TO FINISH THE DISH

**About 30ml garlic oil**
**75 grams pasta**
**About 220ml scampi stock, or as needed**
**50 grams cherry tomatoes, quartered lengthwise and deseeded**
**15 grams uni, divided**
**About 15 garlic chips**
**A few fresh basil leaves**

## METHOD

1 Cut the scampi into large chunks. Heat half the oil in a large, heavy skillet. Add the scampi in batches and fry over a high flame until brown. Use a slotted spoon to remove the scampi from the pan and put into a stock pot.

2 After all the scampi has been browned, add the remaining oil to the skillet. Stir in the leek, fennel, carrot, celery and garlic and cook over a medium flame for about 10 minutes, or until golden. Add the cherry tomatoes, tomato paste and the brandy or cognac. Stir the ingredients thoroughly and cook at a rapid boil until most of the liquid has evaporated. Put these ingredients and the liquid into the stock pot holding the scampi and add the bouquet garni and 1.5 litres of water. Slowly bring the liquid to the boil, then lower the heat. Skim the surface to remove any scum, cover the pan with the lid and simmer for 30 minutes.

3 Remove and discard the bouquet garni. Place a strainer over a clean pan. Pour the scampi stock into the strainer, pressing down on the solids to extract as much flavour as possible. After straining the stock, put the pan over a medium flame and bring the liquid to the boil, then turn off the flame.

4 While the scampi stock is simmering, make the garlic oil and chips. Put the garlic in a small pan with the oil. Heat over a low flame and cook until the garlic is golden brown. Remove the garlic chips from the oil and drain on paper towels.

5 Make the pasta. Bring a pot of heavily salted water to the boil. Heat a skillet and add about 30ml of the garlic olive oil. Add the tomatoes and 220ml of scampi stock and bring to the boil. Dip the pasta in the boiling water for five seconds (just enough to soften it). Drain the pasta and put into the skillet with the tomatoes and scampi stock. Simmer, stirring often, until the pasta is al dente and the stock is absorbed but the mixture is still moist. If the pan becomes too dry before the pasta is cooked, add a little more stock (or boiling water if the sauce is becoming too salty) and continue to cook.

**6** When the pasta is al dente, remove the pan from the heat. Mix 10 grams of the uni in a small bowl, add it to the skillet and stir quickly. Add the garlic chips and basil leaves, stir and put the pasta on a plate. Top with the rest of the uni and serve.

Serves 1.

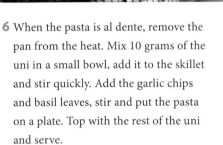 "It's important to add the uni off the heat and stir it quickly or you'll have dry, scrambled uni. The residual heat of the pan cooks the uni and makes it creamy. This part of the recipe can be slightly unforgiving so, if you like, mix a little cream or olive oil into the uni, which will give you a bigger window in which to work." "Don't add oil to the water used to soften the pasta because the pasta will then repel the sauce rather than absorb it."

Cheng says that any leftover scampi stock can be frozen. Leftover garlic oil should be decanted into a bottle and refrigerated.

# SALT-BAKED FISH WITH UNI ROUILLE

*David Lai* majored in art history and fine art at UC Berkeley, before deciding he wanted to cook for a living. He worked under famous chefs Julian Serrano (at Masa's) and Sylvain Portay (at the Ritz-Carlton's Dining Room) in San Francisco, before heading to Monaco for a summer stage (unpaid internship) at Alain Ducasse's Michelin three-star restaurant Le Louis XV. He returned to Hong Kong to help with the 2003 opening of Spoon by Alain Ducasse at the InterContinental in Tsim Sha Tsui. Six years later he started his own restaurant, On Lot 10, in Gough Street, Central, followed by Bistronomique and Boulangerie Bistronomique, both in Kennedy Town.

Lai likes to work with fish and makes daily visits to wet markets to pick the best of the catches, buying local seafood whenever possible. Salt-baked fish has been on the menu of On Lot 10 since the family-style French restaurant opened.

## INGREDIENTS

1 whole fresh fish, about 1kg
20 grams fresh parsley
1kg medium-grain rock salt
About 100 grams egg white
10 grams wakame shreds, soaked in water until soft

FOR THE UNI ROUILLE
1 large egg yolk, at room temperature
50ml extra-virgin olive oil
50ml olive oil
5 saffron threads, soaked in 5ml warm water
10 grams garlic, roughly chopped before being mashed to a paste with the flat side of a knife
A pinch of cayenne or piment d'Espelette
60 grams (or more) sea urchin
Fresh lemon juice, to taste
Fine sea salt

## METHOD

1 Make the rouille. Combine the extra-virgin and olive oils. Put the egg yolk and a pinch of salt in a bowl and whisk to combine. Start adding the olive oil a drop or two at a time, whisking it in thoroughly before adding more. Don't add it too quickly or the mixture will curdle. After a stable emulsion has been established, add the oil in a very thin stream, whisking constantly. As the mixture thickens, add some of the saffron liquid (and strands) before whisking in more oil. After whisking in all the olive oil, stir in the garlic, cayenne or piment d'Espelette, sea urchin and a little fresh lemon juice. Taste for seasonings and adjust as needed.

2 Preheat the oven to 200 degrees Celsius. Rinse the fish inside and out and check that all the innards and scales have been removed. Use paper towels to dry the fish inside and out. Squeeze as much water as possible from the wakame before stuffing the seaweed into the cavity of the fish. Put the salt and parsley in a food processor and pulse until the parsley is finely chopped and blended into the salt. Whisk the egg white and mix it by hand with the salt/parsley; the mixture should be moist enough that when you squeeze it, it will hold its shape. Spread some of the salt on a shallow metal pan just large enough to hold the fish. Put the fish on the salt bed and spread the remaining salt mixture over the fish, pressing on it to encase the fish entirely. Bake at 200 degrees for about 30 minutes. To check if it is done, insert a thin metal skewer into the thickest part of the fish until it almost touches the spine, leave for about 30 seconds, then remove the skewer and place it on your skin just under your lower lip: the skewer should feel hot, but tolerably so. If the skewer is cool or just warm, continue to cook the fish, testing it about every five minutes.

3 When the fish is cooked, remove and discard the salt crust. Serve the fish with the uni rouille on the side.

Serves 2.

---

"The uni flavour in the rouille is very subtle; if you want a stronger uni taste, use less olive oil or add more uni."

"With fresh fish, you should either kill it and cook it immediately, or let it sit for about half a day after it's killed. Otherwise rigor mortis makes the meat too firm."

"A 1kg fish is the ideal size. Farmed fish is usually about 1 catty (approximately 600 grams) and is inferior to wild fish because it doesn't get any exercise."

Lai cooks the fish in a convection oven. In ovens without a fan setting, he suggests placing the salt-covered fish with the tail towards the front of the range, where the heat is less intense.

# SCOTCH EGGS

A friend is on a mission to find the best scotch (although there's nothing Scottish about them) egg in England and samples them whenever she sees them. After she described her idea of perfection - slightly gooey yolk, lightly seasoned meat and a good ratio of meat to egg - I came up with a version. You can make it fancy by adding ingredients to the minced meat mixture, but try it this way first: it's absolutely delicious in its simplicity.

## INGREDIENTS

6 small organic free-range eggs, room temperature
500 grams minced pork
1 tbsp chopped fresh sage
1 tbsp chopped parsley
1 large shallot, finely chopped
Fine dry bread crumbs, for dredging
Fine sea salt and freshly ground black pepper, to taste
Oil, for frying

## METHOD

1 Thoroughly combine the pork with the sage, parsley, shallot and salt and pepper and chill for about 30 minutes.

2 Place the eggs in a pan large enough to fit in one layer without crowding. Cover with cool water. Bring to the boil over a medium flame. Immediately remove the pan from the heat, cover with the lid and allow the eggs to stand for four to five minutes (if you like them hard-boiled, leave them for seven minutes). Pour off the hot water and run the eggs - still in the saucepan - under tap water until they feel cool. Put the eggs in a bowl of iced water. Crack the shells all over, then leave them in the iced water for 15 minutes. Remove the shells and dry the eggs thoroughly. Pack a thin layer of the meat mixture over the eggs to encase them entirely. Dredge in breadcrumbs.

3 Pour oil to the depth of 5cm in a skillet and hear to 180 degrees Celsius. Fry the eggs until medium brown, using a ladle to pour hot oil over them and to turn them over so they cook evenly. Drain on paper towels. Serve hot or warm.

Makes 6.

# PORK SCHNITZEL WITH POTATO SALAD

## INGREDIENTS

8 slices boneless pork loin, about 120 grams each
120 grams plain (all-purpose) flour
1-2 eggs
1/4 tsp paprika
1/2 tsp fine sea salt
1/4 tsp freshly ground black pepper
About 150 grams panko (Japanese breadcrumbs)
Oil, for pan frying
Lemon wedges, for serving
Parsley or chervil leaves, to garnish

FOR THE POTATO SALAD
800 grams fingerling potatoes
250 grams sliced streaky bacon, cut into 1cm-wide pieces
3 large shallots, sliced
1 celery stalk, diced
25 grams grainy mustard
20ml rice wine vinegar
1/2 tsp granulated sugar
About 60ml extra-virgin olive oil
Fine sea salt and freshly ground black pepper

## METHOD

1 Put a sheet of cling film on a work surface. Place a slice of pork loin in the middle of the cling film, then cover it with another sheet of cling film. Use the flat side of a meat mallet to pound the pork as thinly as possible - it should be about 5mm thick. As you pound it, occasionally lift the cling film and smooth it out on both sides of the meat. Repeat with each slice of pork. Place the meat slices - still in the cling-film layers - on a plate, then refrigerate while making the potato salad.

2 Scrub the potatoes but leave the skin on. Put them in a pan and cover with heavily salted cool water. Place over a medium flame and bring to the boil. Lower the heat and simmer the potatoes until just tender enough to be pierced with a fork; do not overcook them. Drain them, then rinse with cold water and drain again. Strip the skin from the potatoes while they are still warm, then cut them into large chunks.

3 While the potatoes are simmering, cook the bacon by putting it into an unoiled skillet set over a medium flame. Cook until the bacon is crisp. Use a slotted spoon to remove the bacon from the pan, then drain it on paper towels. Pour off all but about 60ml of bacon grease from the pan. Put the shallots into the pan and cook over a low flame until soft. In a bowl, mix the mustard with the rice wine vinegar and sugar, then season to taste with salt and pepper. Mix in the bacon, shallots and celery. Add the warm potatoes to the bowl (they absorb the dressing better when they're warm) and mix to coat lightly. Taste for seasonings and adjust as needed. Cover with cling film and set aside while cooking the schnitzel.

4 Put the flour in a shallow pan and thoroughly mix in the paprika, salt and ground pepper. Whisk the eggs in a separate pan and put the panko in a third pan. Heat oil to a depth of 1cm in a skillet set over a medium flame.

5 Dredge a piece of pork in the flour and shake off the excess, then coat it in the beaten egg. Dredge on both sides in the panko and pat the meat gently so the breadcrumbs stick. Fry in the hot oil (about 180 degrees Celsius) for a few minutes on each side, or until golden brown and cooked through. Drain on paper towels.

6 Drizzle the extra-virgin olive oil over the potato salad and mix it in before spooning it onto plates. Place the pork schnitzel on plates, add a lemon wedge to each serving and garnish with parsley or chervil leaves.

Serves 4-8.

# SPARE RIBS WITH PRESERVED PLUMS AND CARAMELISED BLACK VINEGAR

The Chairman has been attracting food lovers almost from the day it opened in 2009; if you want a weekend dinner at this small restaurant in Kau U Fong you might need to book a month in advance. The menu comprises Chinese home-style dishes made with top-quality ingredients and taken to another level, as well as more luxurious creations such as what is arguably the restaurant's most famous dish: steamed fresh flower crab with aged Shaoxing wine and fragrant chicken oil.

*Tin Tang* is a veteran restaurateur; at his peak, he owned almost 40 restaurants in Hong Kong. He retired in 1998 but, dissatisfied with the quality of Chinese restaurants in Hong Kong, opened The Chairman. He wanted, he said, to have a restaurant serving "honest Cantonese food" that was delicate and showed the true flavours of the ingredients.

Tang says his recipe for spare ribs with preserved plums and caramelised black vinegar was inspired by the classic Cantonese dish of pigs' feet with ginger and black vinegar that mothers eat to strengthen their bodies after giving birth. To make it less fatty, he replaced the pigs' feet with ribs, and toned down the sweetness. The finely shredded kaffir lime leaves add freshness. Chef *Kwok Keung-tung* (bottom left, with Tang), who cooked the dish featured, has been at The Chairman since it opened.

## INGREDIENTS

FOR THE MARINADE
**15ml soy sauce**
**2 shallots**
**1 garlic clove**
**A 1.5cm piece of ginger, peeled**
**30 grams carrot**
**30 grams celery**
**1/2 tsp sea salt**
**1 small bunch fresh coriander**
**1 tbsp cornstarch**

TO COOK AND FINISH THE DISH
**500-600 grams meaty pork spare ribs, cut into individual ribs, each about 8cm long**
**120ml Pat Chun sweetened black vinegar**
**3 Chinese dried plums**
**2 slices liquorice root**
**40 grams ginger, peeled and julienned**
**Vegetable oil, for deep-frying**
**2 kaffir lime leaves**

## METHOD

1  Make the marinade. Put the soy sauce, shallots, garlic, ginger, carrot, celery, salt and coriander in a blender and add 60ml water. Blend, then strain out the juice, discarding the solids. Stir the juice with the cornstarch, add the spare ribs, mix thoroughly and leave for two hours.

2  Put the black vinegar, dried plums and liquorice root in a saucepan, bring to the boil, then lower the heat and simmer for 15 minutes. Strain, then discard the solids.

3  Pour oil to a depth of about 10cm in a wok and place over a medium flame. When the oil is about 160 degrees Celsius, fry the spare ribs for about five minutes or until they're cooked through. Increase the heat and fry the ribs until they're golden brown, about one more minute. Drain on paper towels. Pour the oil from the wok and wash it.

4  Pour the vinegar mixture into the wok and heat to simmering with the ginger. Add the spare ribs and stir constantly until the liquid reduces to a glaze that lightly coats the meat.

5  Arrange the spare ribs on a plate. Finely julienne the kaffir lime leaves, sprinkle over the ribs, then serve.

Serves 4 as part of a Chinese meal.

The chefs at The Chairman make all their own sauces, with the exception of soy sauce - and for that, they use Kowloon Soy.

# CHOUCROUTE GARNIE

For the petit salé, use good-quality pork belly: Iberico is ideal; Kurobuta pork belly is too fatty. For the cooked bone-in pork knuckle, buy a smoked or black-pepper version, not honey-roasted.

## INGREDIENTS

**FOR THE SAUERKRAUT**
**1 large head of cabbage**
**Kosher salt or medium-flaked sea salt, as needed**

**FOR THE PETIT SALÉ**
**A 450 gram slab of pork belly**
**400 grams kosher salt or medium-flaked sea salt**
**100 grams granulated sugar**
**The leaves of 2-3 thyme sprigs**

**FOR THE CHOUCROUTE GARNIE**
**About 30 grams duck fat or cooking oil, plus extra for browning the sausages**
**1 medium-sized onion, diced**
**4 garlic cloves, sliced**
**300ml dry white wine**
**500ml unsalted chicken stock, preferably home-made**
**750 grams to 1kg sauerkraut**
**2 or 3 Granny Smith apples**
**6 juniper berries**
**12 whole black peppercorns**
**1 1/2 tsp whole caraway seeds**
**2 bay leaves, torn into small pieces**
**1 cooked bone-in pork knuckle, about 750 grams**
**About a kilo in total of three or four types of fresh sausages (I use Toulouse, garlic and chipolatas)**
**8-12 medium-sized new potatoes**

## METHOD

1  Make the sauerkraut at least a week in advance. Rinse the cabbage and cut into wedges that will fit into the feed tube of a food processor. Cut out and discard the core from the wedges, then shred the cabbage on the finest disc of the food processor. Weigh the cabbage shreds and for each 500 grams, add 15 grams of salt. Mix thoroughly in a large bowl and leave for about an hour, stirring frequently. Pack the cabbage and all the juices into one or two large sterilised glass jars, leaving some room at the top. Press on the cabbage firmly so the liquid starts to come out. Put about 250ml of water into a flexible plastic bag, squeeze out the air and tie the top securely. Put this bag in another plastic bag (in case the first one leaks), squeeze out the air and tie the top. Put this bag directly on the surface of the cabbage in the jar - the liquid in the bag helps to keep the cabbage submerged in the salty brine. Leave the lid of the jar open but put a paper towel over the mouth and secure it with kitchen twine or a rubber band. Put the jar in a cool, shady place (outside, if the weather is cool enough) and leave for a week. Check the sauerkraut occasionally - remove the bag of water and use a sterilised wooden spoon to press the sauerkraut down into the liquid. After a few days it should start to smell fermented and will taste a little sour. When it's sour enough for your tastes, remove the bag of water, seal the jar with the lid and refrigerate until ready to use.

2  Two or three days before making the choucroute, make the petit salé. Cut the pork belly into two pieces, rinse with cold water and pat dry. Find a container that will hold the pork pieces fairly snugly, with about 1.5cm of headspace and about 2.5cm around the edges. Mix the salt, sugar and thyme leaves. Spread some of this mixture in a 5mm-thick layer over the bottom of the container and put the pieces of pork belly on top, placing them so they're not touching each other. Pack the remaining salt/sugar mixture on top, between and around the pork pieces so they're completely surrounded. Put the lid on the container and refrigerate for two to three days.

3  To make the choucroute, put the sauerkraut in a large colander, rinse thoroughly with cold water and drain. Squeeze handfuls of the sauerkraut to remove the excess liquid. Bring a large pan of water to the boil. Add the pork knuckle, bring to the boil, then lower the heat and simmer for about five minutes. Remove the pork knuckle from the water. Scrape the salt from the pork belly

and rinse with cold water. Put the pork belly into the pan of boiling water used to blanch the pork knuckle, then simmer for about five minutes. Drain the pork belly, rinse and drain again. Peel the apples and remove the cores. Cut each apple into eight wedges.

**4** Preheat the oven to 180 degrees Celsius. Heat the duck fat or cooking oil in a very large, heavy pan, preferably enamelled cast iron. Add the onion and garlic and cook over a low flame until soft, stirring often. Add the wine and heat over a medium-high flame until simmering and cook for several minutes. Add the chicken stock and bring to a simmer, then add the sauerkraut, apple, juniper berries, peppercorns, caraway seeds and bay leaf. Stir the ingredients, then add the pork knuckle and petit salé, snuggling them into the pan so they're partly submerged by the sauerkraut. Simmer, then cover the pan, place in the oven and cook for about an hour. Heat some oil in a skillet and brown the sausages, then put them into the pan of choucroute and cook for an additional 30 minutes. Put the potatoes in a pan of salted water, bring to a simmer and cook until they are just tender.

**5** When the choucroute is ready, use tongs to put some of the sauerkraut on a large serving platter. Slice the pork knuckle and petit salé and arrange them, the sausages and potatoes over the sauerkraut. Put the remaining sauerkraut into a bowl and serve hot.

Serves 8-10.

# VIETNAMESE FRIED SPRING ROLLS

I learned from my Vietnamese friends to add Coca-Cola (or another soft drink) to the water into which the rice-paper is dipped - the sugar in the drink caramelises, turning the fried rolls an attractive brown. I like to double-fry the rolls - the first frying cooks the filling while the second (at a higher temperature) makes the exterior crunchier.

If you visit Vietnam, buy the spring-roll wrappers made there; they're much more delicate than the Thai wrappers commonly available in Hong Kong.

## INGREDIENTS

130 grams thinly sliced onion
3 large garlic cloves, minced
300 grams minced pork
300 grams raw shrimp, heads and shells removed, minced
A 50-gram pack of mung-bean vermicelli, soaked in warm water until soft, squeezed dry then chopped
90 grams carrot, roughly grated
25 grams cloud-ear mushrooms, soaked in hot water until soft, squeezed dry then chopped
6 fresh water chestnuts, rinsed thoroughly, peeled and chopped
2 large eggs
30ml Vietnamese fish sauce
1 tsp freshly ground black pepper
Fine sea salt
About 50 small round rice-paper wrappers
1 can Coca-Cola (don't use Diet Coke)
Cooking oil, for frying

FOR THE DIPPING SAUCE AND TO SERVE
120ml Vietnamese fish sauce
30-45ml fresh lime juice
15-30ml rice vinegar
About 15 grams granulated sugar
3-4 garlic cloves, minced
Chopped red chillies, to taste
1 small carrot, finely grated
Cold bottled water, to dilute the sauce
Romaine lettuce leaves
Fresh herbs such as mint and Thai basil

## METHOD

**1** In a large bowl, mix the onion, garlic, pork, shrimp, mung-bean vermicelli, carrot, cloud-ear mushrooms and water chestnuts. Mix in the eggs and season with the fish sauce, black pepper and a little salt.

**2** Cover a baking tray with cling film. Pour the Coca-Cola into a bowl and add an equal amount of cold water. Lay a clean, dry dishcloth on the work surface. Briefly submerge a rice-paper wrapper into the cola/water mixture, lay it on the dishcloth and leave for about 30 seconds, or until it is soft enough to fold without cracking. Spoon some of the filling onto the lower third of the wrapper, fold in the sides and bottom, then roll it up to form a tight cylinder. Put the roll on the baking tray and continue with the remaining wrappers and filling.

**3** Heat cooking oil to a depth of about 1.5cm in a skillet. When the oil reaches 160 degrees Celsius, fry the rolls for several minutes, turning them over once. Fry them in batches. When all the rolls are fried, increase the heat under the skillet so the oil reaches 180 degrees. Fry the rolls again briefly. Drain on paper towels.

**4** Mix the fish sauce, lime juice, rice vinegar and granulated sugar and adjust the seasonings to taste. Dilute the sauce slightly with the bottled water, then mix in the garlic, chilli and carrot.

To eat, wrap the spring rolls in lettuce leaves with the herbs and dip in the sauce.

Serves 8-10 as part of a Vietnamese meal.

# SPIRAL CURRY PUFFS

I usually make curry puffs with home-made flaky pastry but to save time and effort commercial puff pastry works well enough, although it's not as delicate. This filling is adapted from *The Best of Singapore Cooking* by Leong Yee Soo. For a vegetarian version, increase the quantity of peas and substitute diced carrot for the meat, adding it at the same time you add the potato.

## INGREDIENTS

3 sheets (20cm-square) of commercial puff pastry
Plain flour, for rolling
180ml cooking oil, plus extra for deep-frying the puffs
200 grams onion, diced
250 grams potato, peeled and diced
85 grams shallot, thinly sliced
2 large garlic cloves, chopped
15 grams fresh ginger, grated
250 grams minced beef or diced chicken thigh
20 grams curry powder
1/4 tsp cayenne pepper
200ml coconut cream
80 grams frozen peas
Granulated sugar, to taste
Fine sea salt and freshly ground black pepper, to taste

## METHOD

1 Lay the puff pastry squares, slightly overlapping, end to end. Press firmly where they overlap then start at the short end and roll tightly into a cylinder. Wrap in cling film and refrigerate.

2 Heat 90ml of oil in a skillet, add the onion and cook over a low flame until soft and translucent, then transfer to a bowl. Heat 30ml of oil in the skillet (no need to wash it), add the potato and season lightly with salt. Stir to coat the potato with the oil and add about 50ml of water. Cover with the lid, turn the heat to low and simmer until the potato is tender. Increase the heat and cook until most of the water has evaporated. Add the potato to the onion and wash the pan.

3 Heat 60ml of oil in the skillet, add the shallots, garlic and ginger and cook until soft. Add the chicken or beef, season with salt and cook over a medium-high flame to brown the meat. Stir in the curry powder and cayenne, then lower the heat and cook for about five minutes, stirring frequently. If the ingredients stick to the pan, drizzle in a little more oil.

Add the coconut cream and simmer until it has been absorbed but the mixture isn't dry. Add salt, pepper and a little sugar to taste. Stir in the peas and remove from the pan. Allow to cool completely, then refrigerate.

4 Slice the cylinder into 6mm discs and roll each into a 12cm circle. Place two heaped tablespoons of the cold filling in the centre of the circle. Lightly dampen half the circle with water, then fold in half to enclose the filling. Press tightly to seal the edges and crimp them with your fingers. Gently shape each crescent so the centre sticks out slightly - it will look like a misshapen triangle, with the bottom edge slightly curved. Place on a tray lined with parchment paper and refrigerate.

5 Heat the oil in a pan to a depth of about 5cm. When the oil reaches 180 degrees Celsius, fry the curry puffs a few at a time; do not crowd the pan. When they're puffed and golden brown, remove from the oil and drain on paper towels. Serve hot. They can be reheated in the oven at 180 degrees.

Serves 8-10.

# PIGEONS WITH GREEN PEAS, MORELS, BUTTER-ROASTED JAPANESE SWEET POTATOES AND BABY TARO

## INGREDIENTS

2 fresh pigeons, about 450 grams each
3-4 small Japanese sweet potatoes
4 baby taro
45 grams unsalted butter
20 grams dried morels
100 grams diced pancetta
300 grams frozen peas, preferably petits pois
80ml cream
About 40ml cooking oil
Fine sea salt and freshly ground black pepper

## METHOD

1 Chop the wing tips and feet off the pigeon and remove the head and neck, cutting as close to the body as possible. Season the birds inside and out with salt and pepper, then leave at room temperature.

2 Preheat the oven to 200 degrees Celsius. Scrub the sweet potatoes and baby taro but leave the skin on. Put them in a pan that holds them in one layer, cover with hot water from the tap, stir in about 10 grams of salt and place over a high flame. Cover the pot, bring to the boil, then remove the lid, lower the heat and simmer for 10 minutes. Drain the sweet potatoes and baby taro, then put them into a pan that holds them in one layer. Put the butter into the pan and place in the hot oven. As soon as the butter melts, stir the sweet potatoes and taro to coat them in butter. They can roast until all the other ingredienta are ready; stir them occasionally so they cook evenly.

3 Rinse the morels with cold water, then put them in a bowl, cover with warm water and leave to soak. Bring a pot of salted water to the boil, stir in the frozen peas and cook over a high flame for about two minutes. Drain, rinse with cold water and drain again.

4 Over a medium-high flame, heat a heavy, oven-proof skillet, preferably cast-iron. Add the oil and when it's hot, place the pigeons back-side down in the pan. Brown the pigeons well, then turn them over and brown the other side. As the fat renders out, baste the birds with the hot fat to sear the skin. Turn the birds back-side up again.

5 Put the pan of pigeons into the oven and roast for about 10 minutes for rare, to medium-rare. Don't cook them beyond medium or the flavour will become livery. Remove the pan from the oven and leave the birds to rest for 10 minutes.

6 Squeeze the liquid from the morels and cut off and discard the stems. If the morels are large, cut them lengthwise into halves or quarters. Heat a skillet over a medium flame, add the pancetta and cook until it starts to brown. Stir in the peas, morels, cream and salt and pepper to taste. Bring to a simmer and cook, stirring occasionally, until the cream is absorbed.

7 Place the pigeons into the skillet holding the peas and morels. Serve the sweet potatoes and baby taro in a separate dish. The sweet potatoes can be eaten whole; the baby taros should be cut in half, the flesh scooped out and the hairy shells discarded.

Serves 2-4.

# SMOKED CHICKEN

Food writer and art critic *Lau Kin-wai* was at the forefront of the private-kitchen movement in Hong Kong. In 2000 he opened Yellow Door Kitchen, which, like other private kitchens, does not offer a menu: diners eat what the chef cooks. In 2004 the ponytailed writer opened a regular restaurant, Kin's Kitchen, in Tin Hau. But gradually, it's been his son, *Lau Chun* (right), who's been assuming the spotlight. Also a food writer, the younger Lau creates dishes for Kin's Terrace (a private kitchen above Kin's Kitchen), embracing modern equipment such as the sous-vide and Pacojet machines.

But Kin's Kitchen's chicken smoked with rosebuds and sugar cane relies on old-fashioned Cantonese cooking techniques: the whole bird is first poached in master stock, then laid on a rack and smoked. It's so popular that regulars at the restaurant know to order it in advance.

## INGREDIENTS

FOR THE POACHING BROTH

**600 grams yellow rock sugar**
**600ml water**
**300ml light soy sauce**
**4 15cm pieces sugar cane**
**5 bay leaves**
**3 star anise**
**3 whole black cardamom**
**1 cinnamon stick**
**1 fresh chicken (about 1.2kg), innards removed and put to one side**

FOR SMOKING

**30 grams dry rosebuds**
**120 grams yellow slab sugar, broken into large pieces**
**4 15cm pieces sugar cane, cut in half lengthwise**

## METHOD

1 Put the bay leaves, star anise, black cardamom and cinnamon stick in a herb pouch and tie it tightly. Place it in a soup pot, add the rock sugar, water, soy sauce and sugar cane and bring to the boil. Add the chicken and the innards, bring to the boil, then lower the heat and simmer for 20 minutes.

2 Take the chicken and innards from the liquid and place on a rack. Line a wok with a double layer of aluminium foil and place the smoking ingredients on top. Heat the wok over a high flame and when the sugar starts to melt put the rack with the chicken in the wok and cover with the lid. Smoke for five minutes. Cool the chicken briefly and cut it into pieces. Ladle some of the poaching liquid over the chicken and serve.

Serves 6-8 as part of a Chinese meal.

---

The poaching broth can be strained and refrigerated or frozen, then used to cook more chicken, adding sugar, water, soy sauce, sugar cane and herbs as needed. The master stock takes on a richer, deeper flavour the more it's used.

Lau Chun says the sous-vide machine does a better job of making dishes such as Shanghainese drunken pigeon than cooking the bird more conventionally. With the ingredients sealed in an airtight bag the alcohol does not evaporate and cooking it at a precise low temperature ensures the meat isn't overdone.

The Pacojet uses high-speed, razor-sharp blades to shave ingredients to such a degree they can then be strained through a fine sieve to yield intense flavours. Lau uses it to create dishes such as peanut tofu, in which, traditionally, the peanuts were ground with stone mills before being strained.

# YUKHOE

This fast, easy dish (sometimes spelled yukhwe or yukhue) is delicious - if you like raw meat. It takes less time to prepare than the steamed rice to accompany it.

Choose a piece of beef with little exterior fat and silverskin, such as tenderloin or rump. If you're feeling extravagant, make this with wagyu beef. Because the beef and egg yolk are consumed raw, the ingredients need to be pristinely fresh and purchased from a reputable supplier.

## INGREDIENTS

250 grams boneless beef
15ml light soy sauce
10ml pure sesame oil
1 tsp sugar, or to taste
1 garlic clove, crushed
1 tsp sesame seeds, lightly toasted then crushed
Black pepper, to taste
Fresh lemon juice, to taste

FOR THE GARNISH
1-2 spring onions, julienned
1 tsp sesame oil
1/4 tsp Korean chilli powder
1 egg yolk or four quail egg yolks (optional)
20 grams pine nuts, coarsely crushed
Romaine or red leaf lettuce leaves
1-2 garlic cloves, thinly sliced
1/2 Asian pear (nashi), peeled, cored and cut into
thick matchstick pieces

## METHOD

1 Freeze the beef for 30 minutes, then slice into 5mm strips across the grain. Stack the slices and cut them into 5mm strips. Place the meat in a bowl and toss with the soy sauce, sesame oil, sugar, crushed garlic, sesame seeds, black pepper and a squeeze of lemon juice.

2 To make the garnish, toss the spring onion with the sesame oil and chilli powder. Place the beef in the middle of a plate and make a crater in the centre. Place the egg yolk in the crater and sprinkle the crushed pine nuts over the meat. Put the spring onions in a pile on the plate, add lettuce leaves, the sliced garlic and Asian pear.

Serves 2 as part of a Korean meal.

# RASPBERRY, VANILLA-POACHED APRICOT AND GREEK YOGURT PARFAITS WITH LEMON AND MUSCOVADO SUGAR CRUMBLE

You need to bloom (soften in water) the gelatin and melt it into each purée just before using it. If you do it too soon, it might start to set in the bowl, rather than in the glass. Gelatin sheets are a lot easier to use than powdered gelatine, and they're worth looking for.

Choose the yogurt brand carefully. It should be thick but smooth and spreadable, and not too tangy.

## INGREDIENTS

**About 1kg Greek yogurt**

FOR THE RASPBERRY LAYER
**300 grams frozen raspberries**
**200 grams granulated sugar**
**8 grams gelatin sheets**

FOR THE APRICOT LAYER
**500 grams apricots**
**300ml water**
**300 grams granulated sugar**
**1/2 a vanilla bean**
**25ml fresh lemon juice**
**8 grams gelatin sheets**

FOR THE CRUMBLE
**75 grams plain (all-purpose) flour**
**40 grams muscovado sugar**
**1/4 tsp fine sea salt**
**50 grams butter, slightly softened**
**Finely grated zest of half a lemon**

TO SERVE
**Fresh raspberries**
**Fresh mint leaves**

## METHOD

1 Put the raspberries and sugar in a mixing bowl and leave to thaw. Stir the ingredients together until the sugar is dissolved, then purée in a food processor. Leave at room temperature.

2 Halve the apricots and remove and discard the pits, then cut each half into four pieces. Put the sugar and water in a saucepan and stir to dissolve. Split the piece of vanilla bean in half lengthwise and scrape out the seeds. Put the seeds and scraped-out pod into the saucepan. Bring to the boil and add the apricots. Bring to a simmer, then remove from the heat, cover the pan with the lid and leave to poach for 10 minutes, or until they're soft. Drain the apricots in a colander set over a bowl. Purée the apricots in a food processor and weigh the purée. Stir in the lemon juice and add enough of the poaching liquid so the purée weighs 500 grams. Cool to room temperature.

3 Spoon a layer (about 50 grams) of Greek yogurt into eight straight-sided glasses that hold about 240 grams each (if they're bigger or smaller, you'll need to adjust the amount of each ingredient, or make fewer or more of the parfaits). Gently tap the glasses on a dish towel-lined work surface to even out the yogurt layer.

4 Soak eight grams of gelatin sheets in a bowl of cold water so they're submerged. When they're soft, squeeze out as much water as possible, put the gelatin into a bowl then add about 50 grams of the apricot purée. Zap in the microwave for about 20 seconds or until the gelatin is melted but not too hot. Stir well and mix it thoroughly into the remaining apricot purée. Divide the purée among the glasses, spooning it over the yogurt gently so it doesn't disturb the layering. Refrigerate for 30 minutes, or until the purée is set.

5 Spoon a layer of yogurt over the apricot purée, tapping it on the work surface to even it out. Soak eight grams of gelatin sheets in cold water and when they're soft, squeeze them to remove the excess water. Put the gelatin in a clean bowl with about 50 grams of raspberry purée and zap in the microwave as before. When the gelatin is melted stir it into the remaining raspberry purée.

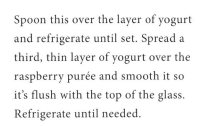

Spoon this over the layer of yogurt and refrigerate until set. Spread a third, thin layer of yogurt over the raspberry purée and smooth it so it's flush with the top of the glass. Refrigerate until needed.

6 Preheat the oven to 180 degrees Celsius. Make the crumble by mixing the flour with the sugar and salt. Cut the butter into small chunks, add them to the flour/sugar and mix with your fingertips until the butter is in very small pieces. Mix in the lemon zest. Take about half the crumble mixture and spread it in a thin layer in a pan. Bake at 180 degrees for about 10 minutes or until brown and fragrant, then allow it to cool. (The remaining crumble mixture can be refrigerated or frozen for another use.)

When it's time to serve dessert, sprinkle some of the baked crumble over the parfaits and garnish with a fresh raspberry and a mint sprig.

Serves 8.

# BANANA CREAM PIE

I came to Hong Kong as pastry chef for The American Pie, a restaurant that was a Lan Kwai Fong institution in the 1990s. This pie was on the dessert list when I arrived, and it was an item we never dared take off the menu because it was so popular.

This is enough dough to make three pies, but enough pastry cream to make two. Freeze the third pastry disc for another occasion. The pie shell can be baked in advance but it tastes best if it's filled and assembled no more than two hours before serving.

The pastry cream recipe is based on one in the book *Mastering the Art of French Pastry* by Bruce Healy and Paul Bugat.

## INGREDIENTS

### FOR THE PIE DOUGH
**360 grams plain (all-purpose) flour**
**1/2 tsp fine sea salt**
**1 tsp granulated sugar**
**250 grams unsalted butter, chilled**
**About 80ml iced water**

### FOR THE PASTRY CREAM
**2 large eggs**
**2 large egg yolks**
**125 grams granulated sugar**
**1/4 tsp fine sea salt**
**35 grams plain (all-purpose) flour**
**35 grams cornstarch**
**500ml whole milk**
**1 vanilla bean**
**50 grams unsalted butter, chilled**

### FOR EACH PIE
**6-8 small ripe Thai bananas (or use three or four regular bananas)**
**About 300ml cream, chilled**
**Chocolate shavings**

## METHOD

1  Make the pie dough first so it has time to chill. Put the flour, salt and sugar in a food processor and pulse to combine. Cut the butter into 1cm chunks, put them in the food processor and pulse briefly, or until the butter is the size of small peas. Put the dry ingredients in a bowl, add the iced water and mix with your hand until it forms a cohesive dough. If it seems dry, add a little more iced water. Briefly knead the dough, then divide it into three even pieces. Shape the dough into a ball, then press on it to flatten into a disc. Wrap each disc in cling film and chill for at least an hour.

2  Put the eggs and egg yolks in a bowl, add the sugar and salt and whisk immediately. Add the flour and cornstarch and whisk until smooth. Pour the milk into a saucepan. Split the vanilla bean in half lengthwise and use a paring knife to scrape out the seeds. Put the seeds and scraped-out pod into the saucepan and set it over a low flame. Bring to a simmer, then turn off the heat. Ladle some of the milk over the egg mixture and whisk immediately. Repeat this twice, then pour the contents of the bowl into the saucepan and whisk. Turn the flame to very low and constantly whisk the ingredients in the saucepan, making sure you scrape the entire interior of the pan so the custard doesn't stick on the bottom and burn. Cook for several minutes so the mixture doesn't taste of raw flour and until the pastry cream is very thick. Scrape the custard through a sieve set over a bowl; discard the vanilla pod. Put the butter into the bowl and, when it melts, whisk it into the custard. Cool to room temperature, then place cling film directly on the surface of the custard (so it doesn't form a skin) and chill.

3  On a lightly floured work surface, roll out the pie dough into a circle that's about 3mm thick and at least 27cm in diameter. Lay it over a 23cm metal pie pan and settle it gently into the contours, taking care not to stretch the dough. Flute the edges of the dough and trim off the excess. Chill for at least 30 minutes.

**4** Preheat the oven to 200 degrees Celsius. Use a fork to poke holes at 1cm intervals in the bottom of the pie crust. Fit a sheet of aluminium foil into the pie shell and fill it with uncooked rice. Bake for 20 minutes, then lift out the foil and the rice. Turn the heat to 180 degrees and bake until the pie shell is completely cooked - it should be pale golden and dry on the surface. If the pastry puffs up as it bakes, gently press it down. Cool completely.

**5** Spread a thin layer of pastry cream into the base of the pie shell. Peel the bananas and lay the fruit in the pie shell, leaving a little space between each banana. Trim the bananas as necessary, so they fit into the shell. Add enough pastry cream to completely cover the bananas. Whip the cream until it forms soft peaks, then put it into a pastry bag fitted with a fluted tip. Pipe the whipped cream on top, then add chocolate shavings. Serve immediately, or within two hours of filling the pie.

Makes 2 pies.

# AFFOGATO

Affogato ("drowned" in Italian) is one of the ultimate pick-me-ups, far more so than tiramisu (whose name translates to "pick me up"). It's easy to make - pour a shot of espresso over ice cream and you have not only a welcome jolt of caffeine, but a lovely contrast between the hot coffee and frozen ice cream, which melts slowly. I'll leave the espresso up to you because everyone likes it their own way - but please don't use instant powder. This recipe requires an ice-cream maker.

## INGREDIENTS

3 large egg yolks, at room temperature
150 grams granulated sugar
1/2 tsp fine sea salt
1 vanilla bean
500ml whole milk
500ml cream
45ml rum, cognac or brandy
Espresso
Chocolate shavings

## METHOD

1 Mix the milk and cream in a saucepan. Split the vanilla bean in half lengthwise and use a paring knife to scrape out the seeds. Put the seeds and scraped-out pod into the saucepan. Place over a medium flame, bring to a simmer, then turn off the heat.

2 In a medium-sized bowl, whisk the egg yolks with the sugar and salt. Add a ladleful of the milk/cream mixture and whisk immediately. Add another ladleful of milk/cream and whisk, then repeat twice more (this heats the egg mixture slowly, so it won't curdle as easily when it's cooked). Constantly whisk the remaining milk/cream as you pour the egg mixture into the saucepan. Place over a low flame and stir slowly but constantly with a wooden spoon. Stir in a back-and-forth motion, scraping the entire bottom of the pan so the mixture cooks evenly and doesn't scramble. The custard mixture is ready when you can draw a track mark with your finger across the spoon. Immediately pour the mixture through a fine sieve into a clean bowl (discard the vanilla pod, or rinse and let dry at room temperature, then put into a container of sugar to make vanilla-scented sugar). Cool the mixture to room temperature, whisking frequently. Whisk in the rum, cognac or brandy, then cover with cling film and refrigerate for about eight hours. Process in an ice-cream machine (you might need to do it in batches), then pack into a container and freeze for at least three hours to allow the flavours to blend and the ice cream to harden.

3 Scoop the ice cream into a coffee cup and pour the espresso over it. Top with chocolate shavings and serve immediately.

Makes at least 12.

# CHOCOLATE AND SALTED CARAMEL TARTS

The chocolate tart dough recipe is from *The Pie and Pastry Bible* by Rose Levy Beranbaum; the caramel and chocolate-glaze recipes are based on ones in Claudia Fleming's *The Last Course*.

If you don't have enough flan rings (this recipe can fill about 20), line the ones you have with dough, bake the shells completely, then remove the rings before lining and baking more. All the baked shells can be filled at once with the caramel and glaze. You can also fill the shells as needed; the caramel and glaze should be warmed gently in the microwave.

Because these tarts are so rich, I make them quite small, using flan rings about 5cm in diameter and 1cm high.

## INGREDIENTS

### FOR THE CHOCOLATE TART DOUGH
180 grams icing sugar
50 grams unsweetened cocoa powder
1/4 tsp fine sea salt
250 grams unsalted butter, chilled
400 grams plain (all-purpose) flour, plus extra for rolling
2 large egg yolks

### FOR THE CARAMEL
400 grams sugar
80 grams light corn syrup
120 grams unsalted butter
120ml cream
30ml crème fraîche

### FOR THE GLAZE
240ml cream
210 grams bittersweet chocolate (65 per cent cacao content), finely chopped
Fleur de sel, for sprinkling

## METHOD

1 Put the icing sugar, cocoa powder and sea salt in a food processor and pulse to combine thoroughly. Cut the cold butter into 1cm chunks, add to the food processor and process until the butter is indistinguishable from the dry ingredients. Add the flour and combine. Whisk the egg yolks and add them to the mixture through the feeding tube with the processor running. Transfer the ingredients to a bowl and finish by hand, kneading briefly into a smooth, cohesive dough. Shape the dough into three discs, wrap each in cling film and refrigerate for at least one hour.

2 Working with one piece of dough at a time, roll it on a lightly floured work surface until it's about 3mm thick. Line the flan rings with the dough, making the edges a little thicker and trimming off the excess at the top of the rings. Put them on a parchment-lined baking tray and use a fork to poke a few holes in the bottom of each shell. Chill for at least 30 minutes.

3 Preheat the oven to 200 degrees Celsius. Place the tray of flan rings in the oven (there is no need to line the rings with foil or use baking weights). Reduce the heat to 180 degrees and bake until the shells are dry and starting to pull away from the sides of the rings. Cool before removing the rings.

4 For the caramel, put the sugar in a saucepan and add the corn syrup and about 150ml of cold water (the exact amount doesn't matter; the water is only to help dissolve the sugar). Place the pan over a medium-high flame and stir occasionally with a wooden spoon until the sugar is completely dissolved. Dip a pastry brush into cold water and wash down all the sugar crystals from the sides of the pan. Cook the mixture without stirring until it turns into a dark amber caramel. Stir in the butter, cream and crème fraîche: it will bubble vigorously and create extremely hot steam so wrap your stirring hand in a dry dishtowel to prevent scalding, and avert your face from the steam. Cool to lukewarm - the mixture should be fairly thick but still liquid enough so it can be spooned into the tart shells. Fill the shells almost to the brim with the caramel and leave at room temperature until firm.

**5** For the glaze, bring the cream to the boil and pour it into a bowl over the chopped chocolate. Allow to stand for a few minutes for the chocolate to melt. Pour most of the cream back into the saucepan (it doesn't matter if some of the melted chocolate goes with it). Start whisking the melted chocolate and add the cream a little at a time to create a smooth, glossy emulsion. Coat each tart with a thin layer of the glaze and leave at room temperature until set. Just before serving, sprinkle each tart with a few grains of fleur de sel. The caramel is slightly gooey at room temperature; it becomes firmer and chewier if refrigerated.

Makes at least 12. The leftover caramel and glaze can be stored in a sealed container in the fridge for at least two weeks.

# DEEP-DISH CHERRY PIE WITH FLAKY CRUST

The ceramic pan I used for this pie held 2kg of fruit and took more than 90 minutes to bake. As with all baked fruit pies, you can tell it's done when the filling starts to bubble out of the crust. The dough for this pie is, ingredients-wise, almost the same as I've used for other types of pie and for quiche. But because I wanted a little more flakiness in the top crust, I've changed the technique.

If the cherries you buy are soft, or if you want a thicker filling, use the larger amount of cornstarch.

## INGREDIENTS

FOR THE CRUST

240 grams plain (all-purpose) flour, plus extra for rolling the dough

120 grams cake flour

1/2 tsp fine-grained sea salt

1 tsp granulated sugar

250 grams unsalted butter, cut into 1cm chunks then frozen for 30 minutes

80ml iced water

1 egg, whisked with 30ml water, for brushing the dough

FOR THE FILLING

2kg fresh black cherries, pitted

200 grams granulated sugar, plus more for sprinkling

1/2 tsp fine sea salt

100-125 grams cornstarch

2 tsp almond extract

60ml fresh lemon juice

## METHOD

1 Put the plain flour and cake flour in the bowl of a food processor, add the sugar and salt, then process to combine. Add the chunks of frozen butter and process until the butter is the size of small peas. Put the ingredients into a bowl and drizzle with the iced water. Mix with your fingertips until roughly combined - there will be damp (but not sopping wet) spots, with some dry spots. Turn the ingredients onto a clean work surface and pat them into a rectangle that's about 24cm by 16cm. With the help of a bench scraper or metal spatula, lift the bottom half of the rectangle and fold it in half so it's 12cm by 16cm. Turn 90 degrees, then pat it out again until it's again 24cm in length. Repeat this twice more; by the time you're finished, the dough will be quite cohesive, with visible streaks of butter. Divide the dough into two uneven pieces - one with about two-thirds of the dough (for the bottom crust), with the remainder for the top crust. Shape the pieces of dough into discs, wrap with cling film and refrigerate for at least an hour (but longer is better; I let the dough rest for at least a day).

Leave the dough at room temperature until it's malleable but still cool. Put the larger disc on a lightly floured work surface, dust it with flour and then roll it out into a large circle that's about 3mm thick. Gently fit the dough over a deep-dish pie pan and settle it gently into the contours, taking care not to stretch the dough. Make a decorative border at the edges and then trim off the excess dough. Chill for at least 45 minutes. Roll out the second piece of dough into a large circle that's 3mm thick. Place the dough on a cutting board (or a parchment paper-lined baking sheet) and chill for 15 minutes. Use a sharp paring knife to cut free-form leaf shapes of different sizes. Separate the "leaves" from the trimmings. Shape the trimmings into a disc, wrap with cling film and refrigerate. Very lightly brush the leaf shapes with beaten egg and score the surface of each one to resemble the veins of a leaf. Refrigerate the leaves. Take the dough trimmings from the fridge, roll them out and cut more leaf shapes, again brushing them with egg and scoring them before putting them in the fridge (you'll need a lot of leaves for the pie).

2 Preheat the oven to 220 degrees Celsius. Lay a sheet of aluminium foil on a baking tray to catch the drips from the pie as it bakes.

**3** Pit the cherries (preferably using a device that removes the pits but keeps the cherries almost whole). Mix the sugar with the salt and cornstarch, then sprinkle this over the fruit and combine thoroughly. Add the almond extract and the lemon juice and mix. Put the filling into the prepared pie shell, mounding it at the centre. Starting from the middle of the pie, and using the largest leaves first, lay the leaves slightly overlapping in a decorative pattern over the filling, sticking them together with a little of the beaten egg. Don't cover the pie entirely; leave several gaps to allow the steam to escape. When the pie is ready, sprinkle it with granulated sugar, then put it on the baking tray and bake at 220 degrees for 15 minutes. Turn the heat to 200 degrees and bake for 30 minutes, turning it around halfway through so it bakes evenly. Turn the heat to 180 degrees and bake the pie for about 50 minutes, or until the filling starts to bubble out of the crust. Again, turn the pie around halfway through. If the top crust starts to get too dark, drape a sheet of aluminium foil over it. Remove the pie from the oven and leave for at least an hour before slicing it into wedges.

Makes 1 pie.

# ASTS

There's no need to reserve feasts just for holidays or festivals. A solo meal can just as easily be a feast, as can an intimate meal with someone you love or an extravagant celebration with friends.

# XO SAUCE

Feel free to vary the proportions of dried scallops and shrimp, as long as the combined weight of dried seafood is about 600 grams. You don't need to use the super-expensive, very large dried scallops, but they should be of reasonable quality; those smaller than 1cm can be tough and chewy. The shrimp should be as small as possible, though; if they're too large, they need to be chopped into tiny pieces, and if they're too hard, you'll need to steam them to soften them.

## INGREDIENTS

500 grams dried scallops

750ml canola or corn oil, plus more as needed

300 grams shallots, minced

12 large garlic cloves, minced

100 grams small dried shrimp

75 grams Yunnan ham, cut into tiny cubes

6-8 red bird's-eye chillies, seeds and stems removed and discarded, then minced

10-20 grams fine chilli flakes

## METHOD

1 Briefly rinse the scallops, then put them in a large heat-proof bowl and steam over simmering water, stirring occasionally. You need to soften them so they're easy to shred; check by pressing on the scallops - they're ready when they start to break apart. Remove the bowl from the heat and break the scallops into thick shreds, removing and discarding any hard parts.

2 Heat about 200ml of oil in a wok, add the shallots and cook over a medium-low flame until soft and translucent. Add the garlic and scallops, and stir in more oil to thickly coat the ingredients. Increase the heat and stir constantly until the ingredients start to sizzle, then lower the heat and add the shrimp, Yunnan ham, bird's-eye chillies and 10 grams of chilli flakes. Stir frequently over low heat (less than a simmer), adding more oil as needed. After about 15 minutes, taste the mixture and add more chilli flakes if it's not spicy enough (err on the side

of caution, though, because the XO sauce's flavour intensifies as it ages in the jars). Continue to cook, stirring frequently, until the mixture is rich, dark and oily.

3 Spoon the mixture into sterilised jars (fill them with boiling water, leave for a few minutes then pour out the water and let the jars air-dry). Press down on the mixture in the jars so the oil rises to the top. There should be enough oil to completely cover the solid ingredients; if needed, pour in a little fresh oil. Cover the jars with sterilised lids, then keep in a cool place for a few days, or refrigerate for longer storage.

# CHAWANMUSHI WITH BLACK TRUFFLE PASTE AND UNI

*Satoru Mukogawa* calls the food he serves at Sushi Kuu "traditional Japanese with a twist". Before moving to Hong Kong, the chef, who hails from Kobe, worked at a Korean-Japanese restaurant in San Francisco, California, where he obligingly made non-traditional dishes, such as California roll and beef roll, for diners who didn't like raw fish.

It was his eagerness to satisfy customers that led to the creation of his versions of the rice burger – unusual items for a restaurant known for its lavish omakase meals. Mukogawa – who is a descendant of samurai (on his mother's side) and sake brewers (on his father's) – said that after Japan's earthquake, tsunami and nuclear disaster in 2011, clientele, worried about radiation poisoning, avoided produce from the country, especially raw fish. The slowdown in business gave Mukogawa time to experiment in the kitchen. Convinced that he could make better rice burgers than those served at fast-food chains in Japan, he came up with variations made with tempura shrimp and wagyu beef.

During this creative period Mukogawa also made chawanmushi with black truffle paste and sea urchin. Although he used sea urchin from Russia, truffles from Italy and eggs from the United States initially, now that fears have subsided he makes the chawanmushi with Japanese ingredients only.

## INGREDIENTS

330ml dashi
20ml mirin
20ml light soy sauce
A pinch of dashinomoto or hondashi
4 free-range eggs
40 grams black truffle paste
30 grams uni

FOR THE 6-1-1
120ml dashi
20ml mirin
20ml soy sauce
A pinch of salt
A little ginger juice (made by grating ginger and squeezing out the juice)
Cornstarch dissolved in water

## METHOD

1 Mix the dashi, mirin, soy sauce and dashinomoto or hondashi and heat until simmering in a pan (this is to evaporate the alcohol in the mirin). Place the pan in a bowl of iced water to cool it quickly.

2 Lightly whisk the eggs and pour through a fine sieve, then stir in the dashi/mirin mixture.

3 Pour the custard mixture into four serving bowls. To rid the mixture of bubbles, use a blowtorch to heat the surface very quickly (which bursts the bubbles). Cover the bowls with their lids.

4 Heat water in the bottom of a tiered steamer and when it boils, put the bowls on the top tier and cover it with the lid. Steam for six minutes, remove the bowls from the steamer and add the truffle paste and uni to each bowl. Steam for two more minutes.

5 While the chawanmushi is cooking make the 6-1-1. Put the dashi, mirin, soy sauce and salt in a saucepan and bring to the boil. Add a little ginger juice and when it simmers lightly thicken the sauce with cornstarch dissolved in water (the sauce should be of a light coating consistency).

When the chawanmushi is cooked ladle some of the 6-1-1 over the top to glaze the ingredients. Put the lids back on the bowls and serve.

Serves 4 as part of a Japanese meal.

---

Mukogawa says that although he makes dashi with a mixture of kombu (dried kelp) and katsuobushi (dried bonito shavings), instant dashi, which is sold in what looks like teabags, can be a substitute. Just follow the directions on the packet.

The chef makes no apologies for using dashinomoto or hondashi, both of which usually contain monosodium glutamate. These ingredients are common in Japanese cooking and, in fact, it was the combination of kombu and katsuobushi that led to the "discovery" of MSG. Japanese scientist Kikunae Ikeda realised that the two ingredients, used together, had a symbiotic, flavour-enhancing effect on foods cooked with them. He isolated the flavour-enhancing "essence" and created what we now call MSG.

6-1-1 refers to the ratio of the main ingredients: six parts dashi, one part light soy sauce, one part mirin.

# MUSHROOM SOUP WITH TRUFFLE OIL AND MUSHROOM TOAST

White truffle oil is best used in very small quantities, so put just a few drops over each portion of soup.

## INGREDIENTS

FOR THE SOUP

About 45 grams unsalted butter
80 grams shallots, finely minced
2-3 large garlic cloves, finely minced
30 grams assorted dried mushrooms (such as chanterelle, porcini or morel)
300 grams assorted fresh mushrooms
60ml sherry
About 1.5 litres unsalted home-made chicken stock
About 200ml cream
Fine sea salt and freshly ground black pepper
White truffle oil and extra-virgin olive oil, to serve

FOR THE MUSHROOM TOAST

Olive oil, as needed
1 garlic clove, thinly sliced
300 grams assorted fresh mushrooms
8 slices sourdough bread (or eight half-slices, if the pieces are very large)
Chopped parsley

## METHOD

1 Briefly rinse the dried mushrooms under running water, then put them in a bowl and add 150ml of warm water. Soak the mushrooms until they're pliable, then strain through a fine sieve set over a bowl. Reserve the soaking liquid and chop the mushrooms. Rinse the fresh mushrooms briefly and pat dry with paper towels before cutting all to about the same size.

2 Heat the butter in a soup pan set over a low-medium flame and, when it's almost melted, add the shallots and cook until soft. Add the garlic and stir for a minute. Turn the heat to high, add the fresh mushrooms and saute until slightly browned. Stir in the sherry and simmer for a few minutes. Add one litre of chicken stock, the soaking liquid and the dried mushrooms. Season with salt and pepper, bring to a boil, lower the heat and simmer for 20 minutes, or until the ingredients are tender. Use a food processor or blender to puree the soup, then pour it back into the pan. Stir in the cream and check the flavour and consistency; if needed, add more chicken stock and salt and pepper. Bring to a simmer and keep it hot.

3 Preheat the oven to 180 degrees Celsius. Brush both sides of the sourdough bread with olive oil and toast in the oven until lightly browned. Rinse the mushrooms, pat them dry with paper towels and cut into even slices. Heat about 20ml of olive oil over a high flame in a large skillet and when it's very hot, add half the mushrooms and half the garlic (don't overcrowd the pan or the mushrooms won't brown and will give off too much liquid). Season with salt and pepper and saute quickly over a high flame until lightly browned. Transfer to a bowl and cook the remaining mushrooms and garlic the same way. Stir the parsley into the mushrooms and spoon over the toast.

4 Ladle the soup into bowls and add two or three drops of truffle oil to each portion. Drizzle some extra-virgin olive oil into each bowl and serve the soup with the mushroom toast.

Serves 8.

# AJO BLANCO WITH GRAPE SORBET AND CROUTONS

This chilled white garlic soup, enriched with ground almonds and bread, is pungent, so don't serve it on a first date. It's traditionally served with peeled grapes, but I can't imagine anything more tedious than peeling grapes. Instead, I serve it with grape sorbet, which is easy to make and delicious (it's also good on its own). Best of all, you don't need to peel any grapes.

## INGREDIENTS

**FOR THE GRAPE SORBET**
300ml water
200 grams granulated sugar
500 grams seedless green grapes
A pinch of fine sea salt
About 45ml fresh lime juice
15ml vodka

**FOR THE AJO BLANCO**
100 grams stale, crustless white bread
About 900ml cold water
150 grams peeled ground almonds
3 large garlic cloves
50ml extra-virgin olive oil, plus extra for drizzling
30-40ml sherry vinegar
Fine sea salt, to taste

**FOR THE CROUTONS**
2 slices stale, crustless white bread
Olive oil, for frying

## METHOD

1 Prepare the sorbet first. Make a sugar syrup by boiling the water and stirring in the sugar. Cool to room temperature and refrigerate. Remove and discard the stems from the grapes. Puree the fruit in a food processor, then put it through the finest disc of a food mill. Weigh the puree, then add sugar syrup in the proportions of three parts puree to two parts syrup (the remaining syrup can be refrigerated and used to sweeten ice tea and lemonade). Whisk in the salt, lime juice and vodka. Chill for several hours, then process in an ice-cream machine. Pack the sorbet into a container and freeze for several hours or overnight.

2 For the ajo blanco, tear the bread into pieces, put in a bowl, drizzle with about 250ml of the cold water, then soak until soft. Put the almonds and garlic in a food processor and purée as smoothly as possible. Add the bread and soaking liquid, then purée again until smooth. With the motor running, drizzle in the olive oil in a steady stream, then add the vinegar and most

of the remaining cold water. Check the consistency and if it's too thick, add more cold water. Season to taste with salt and, if needed, add more sherry vinegar to sharpen the flavour. Strain through the finest disc of a food mill and chill for several hours or overnight. Taste before serving (chilling mutes the flavour) and adjust the consistency if it's too thick.

3 To make the croutons, cut the bread into small cubes. Heat olive oil to a depth of about 8mm in a small skillet. Fry the croutons until golden and drain on paper towels.

Ladle the soup into chilled bowls and drizzle with extra-virgin olive oil. Top with a scoop of the grape sorbet and add a few croutons to each bowl.

Serves about 6.

# HEIRLOOM BEETS WITH YOGURT AND CREAM CHEESE ESPUMA

The Mandarin Oriental's executive chef, *Uwe Opocensky*, considers three pieces of equipment to be essential in a kitchen: a Thermomix, a dehydrator and a Pacojet. The first item is a high-end food processor that also mixes and cooks; the dehydrator desiccates herbs, flowers and other foods to preserve them; and the Pacojet, with its high-speed, spinning super-fine blades, shaves frozen ingredients into ethereal purées.

Before moving to Hong Kong in 2007, Opocensky worked at many restaurants around the world, including the now-closed El Bulli in Spain. He uses several so-called molecular techniques at the Mandarin Grill and the Krug Room. But you won't need special techniques – or a Thermomix, dehydrator or Pacojet – for his heirloom beets with yogurt and cream cheese espuma, a dish that occasionally appears on the menu at the Mandarin Grill.

## INGREDIENTS

2kg heirloom beets
Fine sea salt
Ground white pepper
20ml Manni oil (or another type of extra-virgin olive oil)
10ml balsamic vinegar
5 grams gelatin sheets
250ml apple juice
150 grams feta cheese
50 grams culatello ham, very thinly sliced
16 purple shiso leaves
8 red chard leaves
24 red ribbon sorrel leaves
1 toasted walnut
Freeze-dried beet powder (optional)

FOR THE YOGURT AND CREAM CHEESE ESPUMA
60 grams yogurt
50 grams cream cheese, softened
150ml cream, chilled
25ml milk
1 gram fine sea salt

## METHOD

1 Wash the unpeeled beets and simmer in lightly salted water until tender enough to be pierced with a skewer. Drain them and place in a bowl of iced water for five minutes. Rub off the skin (wear disposable gloves, or the beet juice will stain your hands). Cut the beets into pieces. Opocensky uses cutters to make rounds about 2cm in diameter and about 8mm thick, although you can quarter or halve smaller beets. Season them with a pinch of fine sea salt and ground white pepper, the Manni oil and balsamic vinegar. Purée the trimmings into a smooth mixture in a food processor or blender. Put the purée into a squeeze bottle and refrigerate until ready to serve.

2 Place the gelatin sheets one by one into a bowl of cold water and soak until they're soft. Heat the apple juice to 70 degree Celsius. Squeeze the water from the gelatin sheets and mix them thoroughly with the apple juice. Refrigerate until set, then use a hand mixer to blend until glossy and smooth. Transfer to a squeeze bottle and refrigerate.

3 Whisk together all the ingredients for the yogurt and cream cheese espuma and pass them through a fine sieve. Put the mixture into a siphon fitted with a charger. Shake it well and refrigerate until very cold.

4 To serve, place five to seven dots of the beet puree and apple gel on four large white plates. Break the feta into small, rough pieces and arrange on the plates. Blot the marinated beets with paper towels to remove excess dressing and place them on the plates. Warm the culatello for about five seconds in the oven or under a grill to melt the fat slightly and to release the flavour, then drape and fold the slices around the beets. Put a tiny drop of Manni oil on the shiso, beet blush and sorrel leaves and arrange around the ingredients. Use the siphon to make small white blobs of the yogurt and cream cheese espuma on the plates. Over the ingredients finely grate some walnut with a microplane grater and dust lightly with the beet powder.

Serves 4.

---

It is not essential to use the shiso, beet blush leaves or red ribbon sorrel the recipe calls for. Opocensky says other types of salad greens will do, but suggests choosing small, tender leaves.

Manni oil is a brand of extra-virgin olive oil produced in Tuscany. You can use a different type of extra-virgin olive oil, but the flavour should be delicate.

# SOFT-SHELL CRAB SALAD WITH CANDIED ORANGE PEEL, TOASTED HAZELNUTS AND CITRUS DRESSING

INGREDIENTS

1 orange
100 grams sugar
About 20ml fresh lime juice
120ml extra-virgin olive oil
120 grams mixed greens
25 grams hazelnuts
4 soft-shell crabs, thawed, if frozen
40 grams plain (all-purpose) flour
40 grams cornstarch
Paprika and cayenne pepper
Fine sea salt and freshly ground black pepper
Oil, for frying

## METHOD

1 Make the candied peel. Cut off the top and bottom of the orange, slicing just deep enough to expose the flesh at both ends. Stand the orange on a flat end and use a small serrated knife to remove the rind from the fruit in wide slices, cutting just down to the flesh and following the curve of the orange. When you have finished, you'll have a pile of orange peel and a "naked" orange. Trim the pieces of peel into neat, evenly thick pieces, then cut into 5mm-wide slices. Put the peel into a small pan of water, bring to the boil, then drain in a colander. Put fresh water into the pan, add the peel, bring to the boil and drain. Repeat this process two more times - this removes some of the bitterness from the peel. Put 200ml of fresh water into the pan, add the sugar and stir to dissolve. Add the peel, bring to the boil over a medium flame, then reduce the heat and simmer until the rind is tender. Cool to room temperature. Take about three slices of the candied peel and rinse under cold water to remove the excess syrup. Pat them dry with paper towels and dice. The remaining peel can be stored (in the syrup) at room temperature or in the fridge.

2 Supreme the skinned orange: hold the fruit in one hand and use a small serrated knife to cut out the segments of fruit between the membranes. After removing the orange segments, squeeze the remaining juice from the membranes and discard the membrane.

3 Preheat the oven to 180 degrees Celsius and toast the hazelnuts until they're fragrant and golden brown. Rub the hazelnuts between the palms of your hands to loosen the skin. Roughly chop the skinned hazelnuts.

4 Make the dressing by whisking 20ml of the orange juice with the lime juice, olive oil and salt and pepper to taste. Add more lime juice if it is too sweet.

5 Use kitchen scissors to trim off the eyes and mouth of the crabs. Turn each crab on its back and find the flap at the base: lift it then pull it off. Turn the crab over. Lift the top shell on the left side of the crab, folding it over towards the centre to expose the feathery lungs. Pull out and discard the lungs, then do the same on the right side of the crab. Dry the crabs with paper towels.

6 Mix the cornstarch and flour and season with salt, pepper, paprika and cayenne pepper. Heat oil to a depth of about 2cm in a skillet. Thoroughly dredge each crab in the flour-cornstarch mixture, making sure they are entirely covered, and also flour the crabs under the top shell and where the lungs were. Shake off the excess flour and fry the crabs in hot (180 degrees) oil until they are cooked through (about two minutes on each side). Drain on paper towels.

7 Pile the salad greens onto four plates and drizzle with some of the dressing. Add the toasted hazelnuts, the orange segments and candied orange zest before topping with the soft-shell crabs.

Serves 4.

# SNAPPER WITH BABY SPINACH

*Umberto Bombana*, known as a "white truffle ambassador", came to the notice of Hong Kong food lovers when he was chef at Toscana in the Ritz-Carlton. Two years after the hotel closed in 2008, he opened Otto e Mezzo in Alexandra House, Central.

As part of the restaurant's set lunch, Bombana serves this easy but elegant snapper with baby spinach, which is so popular he can't take it off the menu. He describes it as carpaccio in style because the fish is sliced very thinly. It's cooked briefly so it remains moist.

## INGREDIENTS

280 grams sashimi-grade snapper, chilled
Extra-virgin olive oil, as needed
1 tbsp dried breadcrumbs
A few leaves of fresh oregano
120 grams baby spinach leaves, thoroughly rinsed and dried

FOR THE DRESSING AND GARNISH
15ml fresh lemon juice
30ml extra-virgin olive oil
Orange zest, finely grated
A few capers, chopped
Fine sea salt and freshly ground black pepper
2 cherry tomatoes

## METHOD

1 Preheat the oven to 220 degrees Celsius. Lightly oil four pieces of parchment paper. Cut the snapper into very thin slices and lay them, slightly overlapping, in a circle (about 15cm in diameter) on the parchment. Season lightly with salt and pepper and drizzle with extra-virgin olive oil. Spread the oil over the fish to coat it lightly but evenly. Sprinkle with breadcrumbs and add a few oregano leaves. Place the fish in the oven and bake for 30 seconds, cooking it just long enough to turn the fish white, rather than opaque.

2 Heat about 15ml extra-virgin olive oil in a skillet, add the spinach leaves, sprinkle with salt and cook briefly so the leaves are slightly wilted. Drain the spinach, divide into four portions and place on plates.

3 Use a wide metal spatula to lift the fish from the parchment and place it over the spinach. Mix the lemon juice and 30ml extra-virgin olive oil and drizzle over the fish. Grate orange zest directly onto the fish and add some chopped capers. Cut the cherry tomatoes in half and top each portion with a piece before serving.

Serves 4 as a starter.

"This is a good dinner-party dish because it doesn't take very long to prepare. Because it's such a simple dish, you need the best ingredients. I use the kind of snapper that Japanese chefs would use to make sashimi. Don't cook it too much – just warm it through, or it will be too dry. Even the spinach should be almost raw – don't overcook it."

"The amount of lemon juice and extra-virgin olive oil can be adjusted to suit your tastes. Lemon and olive oil is a classic dressing; I add capers and orange zest to give it more flavour."

"I try to use the best ingredients in the world – Japanese tuna, Italian tomatoes, Japanese snapper, Spanish jamon – as long as it tastes great. I'm not going to stop using the best just because it's not Italian. The pata negra de bellota is much better quality than Parma ham. Parma ham is more of a daily food; it's more casual – and it costs one-quarter the price."

# CITRUS, FENNEL AND AQUAVIT-CURED SALMON WITH LEMON-HORSERADISH SOUR CREAM

The curing time varies according to how strongly flavoured you want the fish to be. After about 12 hours, the salmon is "cooked" enough: the texture will be soft and the flavour quite mild. If you leave it longer, the salmon becomes firmer and the taste saltier. I wouldn't cure it for more than 1 1/2 days.

## INGREDIENTS

600 grams skin-on salmon fillet, in one piece, and about 2.5cm thick at its thickest part
150 grams kosher salt (or another type of medium-grained salt)
150 grams granulated sugar
Finely grated zest of one lemon, one orange and two limes
24 whole black peppercorns, lightly crushed in a mortar
1 tbsp lightly toasted fennel seeds, crushed
About 30ml aquavit (or vodka)

FOR THE LEMON-HORSERADISH SOUR CREAM
200 grams sour cream
Finely grated zest of one lemon
About 25 grams fresh horseradish, grated

TO SERVE
Rye or pumpernickel bread, thinly sliced
Fresh fennel or dill sprigs
Lemon wedges

## METHOD

1 Rinse the salmon fillet with cold water, drain it and pat it dry with paper towels. Run your fingers over the fleshy side of the salmon to check for bones, remove any you find with needle-nose pliers. Thoroughly combine the salt, sugar, citrus zest, peppercorns and fennel seeds. Add just enough aquavit (or vodka) to moisten the ingredients. Lay a sheet of cling film on the work surface. Spread an even layer of some of the salt/sugar mixture - about the same surface dimensions of the salmon - on the cling film. Put the salmon skin-side down on top of the salt/sugar mixture, then cover with the remaining mixture so the fish is completely encased in it. Wrap the cling film tightly around the fish and place on a dish large enough to hold it (in case it leaks). Refrigerate for at least 12 hours and up to 36 (you can unwrap the fish occasionally during the curing process and cut off a piece to taste whether it's the way you want it). When the salmon is ready, unwrap it and scrape away all the curing ingredients. Rinse it briefly with cold water and pat it dry with paper towels.

2 Mix the sour cream with the lemon zest and horseradish to taste (the flavour will increase the longer it stands). Slice the cured salmon across the grain into thin pieces. Spoon a dollop of the sour cream mixture onto the bread and drape a piece of the salmon over it before garnishing with fennel or dill and adding a squeeze of lemon.

Serves 6-8.

# CRAB TIRAMISU WITH FRUIT AND TANDOORI SPICES

*Vincent Thierry* has been at the helm of Caprice at the Four Seasons Hotel Hong Kong since its opening in 2005, coming here from Le Cinq at sister property the Four Seasons Hotel George V, Paris.

For this dish of crab tiramisu, Thierry uses French tourteau crab, and a square mould for neat layers, although the shape of the receptacle can vary to include even Martini glasses. Thierry uses a siphon for the mascarpone layer; if you don't have one, chill the mixture, then whip it.

## INGREDIENTS

FOR THE CRAB GLAZE AND MASCARPONE
SIPHON
600ml crab stock (see method below)
400ml veal stock (see method below)
200 grams mascarpone cheese
120ml cream
2 egg yolks
60ml milk

FOR THE CRAB AND THE FRUIT WITH
TANDOORI SPICES
500 grams crab meat
10 grams shallots, minced
50ml lemon vinaigrette (using one part lemon
juice and three parts extra-virgin olive oil)
5 grams chives, minced (don't use Chinese
chives)
Fine sea salt and freshly ground black pepper
10 grams paprika
40 grams tandoori chicken masala (available
at shops that sell Indian products)
10ml water
50 grams plain yogurt
800 grams mango
400 grams papaya
50 grams roasted piquillo pepper
10ml white balsamic vinegar

FOR THE GARNISH
Minced chives
Tandoori chicken masala
Crab glaze
Piquillo peppers, puréed until smooth and
put in a squeeze bottle

## METHOD

1 Combine the crab and veal stock in a saucepan, bring to the boil, lower the heat and simmer until it's reduced to a good glazing consistency. Season to taste with salt and pepper. Put about 100ml of the glaze in a squeeze bottle and set it aside for decorating the plate.

2 Whisk the mascarpone and cream until smooth and refrigerate. In a bain-marie set over a pan of simmering water, whisk the egg yolks with the milk and remaining crab glaze. Whisk constantly until the mixture reaches 82 degrees Celsius. Allow to cool, then whisk in the mascarpone-cream. Transfer the mixture to a siphon fitted with a gas charger. Refrigerate until very cold.

3 Mix the crab meat with the shallots, lemon vinaigrette and chives. Season to taste with salt and pepper.

4 Mix the paprika with the tandoori chicken masala and stir with water until it forms a smooth paste. Stir in the yogurt.

Peel the mango and papaya and dice finely. Reserve some of the diced mango for the garnish. Dice the piquillo pepper and stir in the balsamic, then combine with the papaya and remaining mango. Thoroughly mix these ingredients with the spiced yogurt.

5 To assemble the dish, place a 12cm square mould in the middle of a plate. Spoon some of the crab mixture into the base of the mould and smooth the surface. Cover with a layer of the marinated fruits. Use the siphon to add the top layer of mascarpone, then smooth the surface so it's flush with the edge of the mould. Sprinkle with minced chives and dust very lightly with tandoori chicken masala. Carefully remove the mould. Repeat nine times to make 10 portions. Decorate the plates with dots of crab glaze and piquillo pepper coulis and add a few pieces of diced mango.

Serves 10.

For the crab stock, wash 1kg of fresh crabs and lightly crush the shells. Put the crabs in a pot with 100 grams chopped onion, 50 grams diced carrot, 50 grams chopped leek, 10 grams chopped celery, 2 garlic cloves, the zest of half an orange and the zest of half a lemon. Cover with water, bring to the boil, lower the heat and simmer for an hour. Strain out the solids, then reduce the liquid until the flavour is intense. Any remaining stock can be frozen for future use.

For the veal stock, roast 4kg of veal bones in the oven at 225 degrees Celsius. Put the bones in a large soup pot with 200 grams chopped onion, half a leek, 2 carrots, 1 celery stalk, half a head of garlic, 1 bay leaf, 1 thyme sprig and 80 grams tomato paste. Cover with water, simmer, turn the heat to very low and cook for 24 hours. Strain out the solids, then reduce the liquid. The remaining stock can be frozen for future use.

# CRAB, ASPARAGUS AND SAFFRON TARTS

All the components of this dish can be prepared in advance: partially bake the tart shells; blanch the asparagus, mix it with the crab meat and put it in the fridge; and whisk together the custard. About 40 minutes before serving the tarts, preheat the oven, fill the shells with the crab/asparagus mixture, pour in the custard and bake.

## INGREDIENTS

### FOR THE PÂTE BRISÉE
**180 grams plain (all-purpose) flour**
**1/4 tsp fine sea salt**
**1/2 tsp granulated sugar**
**125 grams unsalted butter, chilled, cut into 1cm chunks**
**About 30ml iced water**

### FOR THE FILLING
**140 grams canned crab meat**
**6-8 thin asparagus spears**
**10ml cooking oil**
**1 small shallot, minced**
**1 small garlic clove, minced**
**A pinch of saffron threads, soaked in 15ml boiling water**
**Fine sea salt and freshly ground black pepper**
**3 egg yolks**
**270ml cream**

## METHOD

1 To make the pâte brisée, put the flour, salt and sugar in a food processor and pulse to combine. Add the chunks of butter and pulse until they're the size of small peas. Transfer the ingredients to a bowl and add just enough iced water to create a dough that's neither sticky nor dry. Knead briefly and shape into a disc, wrap in cling film and refrigerate for one hour. On a lightly floured work surface, roll out the dough so it's about 3mm thick. Cut the dough into four pieces and fit gently into individual tart pans with removable bottoms about 8cm in diameter and about 2cm deep. Use a fork to poke holes in the bottom crust and chill for 30 minutes. Preheat the oven to 200 degrees Celsius. Cut four squares of aluminium foil large enough to fit in the tart pans with some overhang. Press the foil over the dough in the tart pans and add uncooked rice to act as a weight so the crust doesn't puff up. Place the shells on a baking tray. Bake at 200 degrees for 10 minutes, then reduce the heat to 180 degrees and cook for five minutes. Remove the rice and the foil and continue to bake the tart shells for about five more minutes, or until they're partially baked and starting to turn pale gold. Let the tart shells cool to room temperature. If baking the tarts immediately, leave the oven on.

2 To make the filling, cut off 4cm tips of four asparagus spears and cut them in half lengthwise. Cut the remaining asparagus into 5mm-thick rounds. Bring a pan of salted water to the boil and blanch all the asparagus for 30 seconds. Drain, rinse with cold water, drain again and mix the rounds with the crab.

3 Heat the oil in a skillet, add the shallot and cook over a low flame until soft. Add the garlic and cook for about 30 seconds. Stir in the saffron and soaking liquid, bring to the boil then cool to room temperature.

4 Whisk the egg yolks with the cream, add salt and pepper to taste, then stir in the shallot/saffron mixture. Put the asparagus rounds and the crab meat into the four tart shells. Carefully pour in the custard mixture and top with the reserved, halved asparagus tips. Bake at 180 degrees for about 20 minutes, or until the custard is set and just starting to puff. Serve warm or at room temperature.

Makes 4 tarts.

# OOLONG TEA-SMOKED DUCK EGGS WITH BLACK TRUFFLE PASTE

The Hotel Icon in Tsim Sha Tsui has such professional staff that it's hard to believe it's the training ground for future hoteliers. At times it can be difficult to tell the students from the paid staff. The hotel serves as a teaching and research establishment for The School of Hotel and Tourism Management at the nearby Hong Kong Polytechnic University.

The quality is nowhere more noticeable than in Above & Beyond, the restaurant and bar at the top of the hotel. Sir Terence Conran's design for the venue makes the most of a bird's-eye view of Victoria Harbour and Hong Kong Island. But it's the modern Chinese food by *Joseph Tse* that's the real draw. In pristine whites, the tall chef strolls around the dining room to talk to customers at every table. Noticing that many of them enjoyed smoked dishes, he came up with a delicious appetiser of tea-smoked eggs with black truffle paste. The chef says he used his staff to test versions of it and when at least 80 per cent gave the thumbs up, he knew it would be a success and put it on the menu.

## INGREDIENTS

10 duck eggs, at room temperature
1 gram oolong tea leaves
10 grams plain (all-purpose) flour
5 grams uncooked rice
10 grams crushed slab cane sugar
Dark soy sauce, for coating the eggs

TO FINISH THE DISH
Pepper salt (finely ground white pepper mixed with fine sea salt)
Black truffle paste
Chives, finely minced (don't use Chinese chives, because the flavour is too strong)

## METHOD

1 Fill a bowl with cold water and lots of ice cubes and set it aside. Thoroughly rinse the duck eggs and put them in a pan that fits them in one layer, with just a little room to spare. Cover with cool tap water to about 1cm above the eggs. Place the pan over a high flame and bring to the boil as quickly as possible, using a kitchen timer to cook the eggs for six to eight minutes. Remove the pan from the heat, cover with the lid and let the eggs poach for one to two minutes. Take them from the hot water and put them into the bowl of iced water. Leave the eggs for a few minutes to cool, then crack the shells but leave them in the water for about two more minutes (cold water between the shell and the egg makes peeling easier). Peel the eggs, dipping them in the cold water if the shell is tightly stuck.

2 Mix the tea leaves, flour, rice and sugar and scatter on the bottom of a clean, dry wok. Coat the eggs in soy sauce and place them in a shallow bowl that holds them in one layer. Place the bowl on a rack set in the wok, then cover the wok with the lid. Turn the flame to high. The smoke that comes out of the wok will be white at first, then a pale yellow. Remove the eggs from the wok as soon as the smoke turns dark yellow.

3 Use a very sharp, thin knife to halve the eggs, placing each half in a porcelain soup spoon. Sprinkle a little pepper salt over each half and top with a dab of the black truffle paste. Scatter minced chives over the eggs and serve.

Serves 10 as part of a Chinese meal.

---

It might take a few attempts to perfect the timing so the egg white is just firm enough to hold the yolk, which should be oozing. In chef Tse's super-powerful wok, in which water boils in less than 60 seconds, the eggs were ready in precisely six minutes from the time he turned on the heat to when he removed them from the wok. On my much weaker home stove, the eggs took eight minutes to cook (starting from when I turned on the heat), plus two minutes of resting time in the hot water. It's important to use a pan just large enough for the number of eggs; if they have too much room, the water will take longer to heat and they'll be undercooked. The eggs should be at room temperature before being cooked.

Tse says he uses duck eggs for this dish because they have more flavour and a richer, oilier yolk than chicken eggs.

Don't oversmoke the eggs or they'll taste bitter.

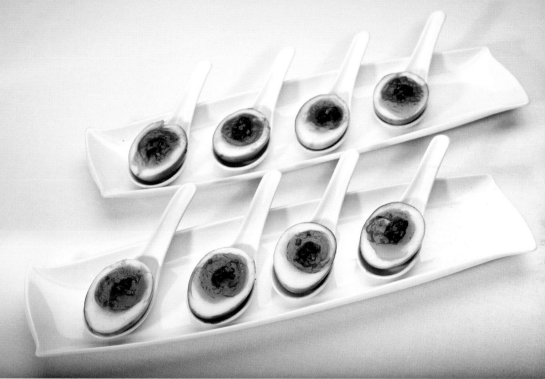

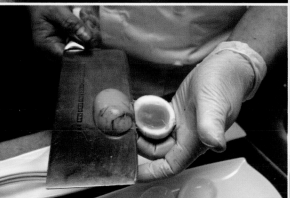

# MISO-MARINATED BLACK COD IN HOBA LEAF WITH PICKLED YOUNG JAPANESE GINGER

*Sebastien Lepinoy* came to Hong Kong as executive chef of L'Atelier de Joel Robuchon at the Landmark, Central, and is now chef de cuisine at Cépage in Wan Chai. Although his cuisine is unmistakably French, it has started to take on more than just a hint of Japanese influence.

The reason, Lepinoy says, is that he prefers Japanese to French ingredients because they are fresher. "I can place an order [with Japanese suppliers] at night and they're delivered the next morning by 7am," he says. "With French ingredients, I order a week in advance and they arrive about a week later."

For this dish of miso-marinated black cod, Lepinoy uses the hoba leaf for aesthetic reasons. In Japan the leaf was originally used to wrap fish so it could be transported inland from the sea. Cod thus wrapped was then cooked in the leaf, with the miso marinade helping as a preservative.

There's no need to use all the marinade at once: Lepinoy says that it will keep refrigerated for up to a month.

## INGREDIENTS

125ml sake
125ml mirin
50 grams red miso
250 grams white miso
125 grams brown miso
75 grams granulated sugar
8-10 pieces (60 grams each) black cod
Oil, for the pan
8-10 hoba leaves
8-10 pieces pickled young Japanese ginger (available in shops that specialise in Japanese ingredients)
Gold leaf (optional)

## METHOD

1 Bring the sake and mirin to the boil (this cooks off most of the alcohol) in a large pan. Add the sugar and the three types of miso and whisk until smooth. Simmer over a very low flame for 10 minutes, then allow the marinade to cool. Slather the marinade over the cod, cover with cling film and refrigerate for at least two days.

2 Scrape the excess marinade off the cod before putting the fish on a lightly oiled metal pan. Place under a hot grill and cook for seven to eight minutes.

3 If using gold leaf, drape a piece of it over the fish, pressing lightly so it adheres. Wrap the fish in a hoba leaf, piercing the leaf with the firm stem to secure it.

4 Garnish with the pickled young Japanese ginger and serve.

Serves 8-10.

---

Lepinoy mixes three types of miso from Kyoto for the marinade because, he says, the different varieties – sweet, spicy and salty, for example – combine to create greater balance. He advises using top-quality rather than mass-produced miso.

# SALT-ROASTED LANGOUSTINES WITH ROASTED CHERRY TOMATOES, WHITE WINE, ARUGULA AND SQUID-INK PASTA

Don't use an expensive brand of coarse salt for this dish; buy the cheapest you can find at a supermarket.

## INGREDIENTS

4-6 langoustines, thawed, if frozen
Coarse salt, as needed
Egg whites, as needed
250 grams cherry tomatoes, halved
1 small thyme sprig, leaves only
40ml extra-virgin olive oil, divided
30ml cooking oil
2 shallots, sliced
2 garlic cloves, sliced
1/4 tsp chilli flakes, or more to taste
100ml dry white wine
30 grams unsalted butter
Fine-flaked sea salt and freshly ground black pepper
200 grams squid-ink pasta
A handful of arugula

## METHOD

1 Preheat the oven to 220 degrees Celsius. Spread a 1cm-thick layer of rock salt on a baking tray that will fit them in one layer. Briefly rinse the langoustines and dry them with paper towels. Put the langoustines close together in one layer on the salt and drizzle them with 20ml extra-virgin olive oil. Mix more of the salt with just enough egg whites so it holds together when squeezed. Spread this over the langoustines, then press on it to make it compact.

2 Put the cherry tomatoes in one layer on another baking tray, drizzle them with the remaining olive oil, sprinkle lightly with fine-flaked sea salt and add the thyme leaves. Mix the tomatoes to coat them with the oil and arrange them so they are cut-side up on the baking tray. Put the langoustines and tomatoes in the oven. The langoustines should cook for 10 minutes, the tomatoes until they're slightly shrivelled and starting to brown in spots. Leave the langoustines for 10 minutes at room temperature, then carefully crack off the salt (it's very hot, so take care). Brush away as much salt as possible from the langoustines, then crack the claws slightly with a meat mallet.

3 While the langoustines and tomatoes are cooking, start boiling the pasta in a large pot of salted water. Try to time it so the pasta and sauce are ready at the same time.

4 Heat the cooking oil in a large skillet, add the shallots and garlic and cook until soft and translucent. Add the chilli flakes and cook for about 30 seconds, then add the white wine. Bring to the boil, then simmer until it's reduced by half. Add the langoustines and the tomatoes with their juices and simmer briefly.

5 When the pasta is al dente, drain it briefly but do not rinse, then add it to the skillet. Season to taste with salt and pepper. Turn off the heat, add the butter and mix thoroughly until it melts. Add the arugula and mix. Divide the ingredients between two plates, putting the langoustines on top, then serve.

Serves 2.

# PIPA DOUFU

*Cheng Kam Fu* worked as a private chef for local tycoons and exclusive clubs before striking out on his own and opening Celebrity Cuisine in the Lan Kwai Fong Hotel, Central, in 2007. The name of the restaurant became a self-fulfilling prophecy and quickly attracted famous clientele, snapshots of whom you will see in a photo album by the entrance. Cheng excels at home-style Cantonese classics and visits fresh-food markets twice a day to search for the best seafood and other produce.

Cheng's dish is on the English menu as "stewed minced assorted meat with beancurd" but is perhaps better known as pipa doufu because the steamed, then fried, beancurd fritters are said to resemble the four-stringed musical instrument. The chef says that pipa doufu is often served with a sauce, but his version needs no accompaniment because it is crisp and full of flavour.

## INGREDIENTS

350 grams soft beancurd, drained, then cut into 5mm dice
70 grams mud carp, minced to a paste
20 grams Jinhua ham, very finely minced
20 grams shallots, minced
A small handful of fresh coriander leaves, chopped
A pinch of sugar
1 egg white
A heaped tsp of cornstarch, plus more for dusting
Fine sea salt and finely ground white pepper
Oil, for frying

## METHOD

1 Thoroughly mix the mud carp with the ham, shallots, coriander, sugar, egg white, cornstarch and some salt and pepper, then gently fold in the beancurd.

2 Use six to eight Chinese porcelain spoons to scoop up the mixture, mounding it slightly over the spoons. Heat water in the bottom of a tiered steamer and when it boils, arrange the spoons on a plate and place it in the steamer. Cover the steamer with the lid and cook the beancurd mixture for seven minutes. Remove the spoons from the steamer and allow to cool.

3 Pour oil to a depth of about 6cm in a wok or skillet. Carefully remove the steamed beancurd mixture (which will be very delicate) from the spoons and lightly dust each one with cornstarch. When the oil is hot, add the beancurd quenelles and deep-fry them for two to three minutes, or until golden. Drain them briefly on paper towels, then arrange on a plate and serve.

Serves 6-8 as part of a Chinese meal.

# NOR MAI GAI

Use a small chicken for this dish; a large one would be harder to handle and cook. Water chestnut flour gives the best crunch but cornstarch can be substituted. Tunnel-boning the chicken is more difficult to describe than it is to perform. When you're done, the only bones left will be the drumette part of the wing (you'll cut off the other two wing joints) and the tip of the drumstick.

## INGREDIENTS

1 small chicken, about 1kg
Soy sauce, as needed
Water chestnut flour or cornstarch, for dredging
Oil, for frying

FOR THE NOR MAI FAN
360 grams glutinous rice
200 grams long-grain rice
1 tsp fine-grained sea salt, plus extra for sprinkling
30 grams dried shiitake mushrooms
30 grams dried shrimp
4 laap cheong (Chinese air-dried sausages)
250 grams char siu (barbecued pork)

## METHOD

1 Wash the glutinous and long-grain rice until the water runs clear. Mix in the salt, add enough water to cover by 2cm and soak for at least eight hours. Put the rice in a rice cooker. Add more water to cover the rice by 1cm and cook until tender. Check the rice periodically and add more water if needed.

2 Rinse the mushrooms and dried shrimp and soak in warm water to cover for about 30 minutes, or until the mushrooms are soft. Drain, then squeeze as much water as possible from the mushrooms. Remove and discard the stems, then dice the caps. Steam the laap cheong for 10 minutes, then dice. Dice the char siu. When the rice is cooked, mix in the mushrooms, shrimp, laap cheong and char siu. Spread on a lightly oiled baking tray and cool to room temperature.

3 To tunnel-bone the chicken, cut off the tip and middle joint of both wings. Place the bird on the cutting board with the neck-side up. Feel around in the cavity for the wishbone, then use a paring knife to scrape the flesh from it. Snap it from the carcass at the base of the "V" and pull it out of the cavity. Grasp the wing and wiggle it around to feel where the drumette bone meets the shoulder, then use a knife to cut between the joint within the cavity. Repeat on the other side.

4 Scrape away the flesh from the collarbone and shoulder bones on one side of the carcass. Break the bone at the point where it meets the carcass and pull the bones from the cavity. Repeat on the other side. Put the bird, breast-side up, on the cutting board. Carefully scrape away the flesh from the breast as close to the carcass as possible. When you are about halfway down, snap the breastbone in two and pull out the top half. Start working on the back part of the carcass, again scraping away the flesh as close to the bone as possible (the flesh is very thin along the backbone). When you are halfway down the back, snap it in two between the vertebrae and pull out that part of the backbone. Continue working on the breast side until you're able to pull out the remainder of the breastbone, then finish with the back. When you come to the point at which the back meets the thigh, carefully cut between the joint. Cut off the backbone at the tail (leave the tail intact) then pull out the last of the backbone. The chicken will be inside-out at this point. Scrape away the flesh from the thigh bone until you reach the drumstick, cut between the joint and remove the thighbone. Cut the tendons at the top of the drumstick and scrape the flesh down the length of the bone until you reach the tip. The drumstick will be turned inside out. Use a sharp, heavy knife to break the drumstick bone

as close to the tip as possible and remove it. Sprinkle salt evenly over the interior flesh. Turn the bird right-side out and sprinkle salt over the skin.

**5** Stuff the chicken with the glutinous rice, pushing it well into the drumstick and thigh parts. Within the cavity, the layer of rice should be about 3cm thick. (Any excess filling can be eaten on its own; reheat it by pan-frying until crusty.) Use toothpicks or skewers to "sew" up the openings at the neck and tail. Place the bird, breast-side up on a rack with low feet and small enough to fit in a wok. Pour water into the wok and bring to the boil. Place the chicken (on the rack) in the wok, cover and steam for 15 minutes. Remove the bird (still on the rack) and cool for 15 minutes. Refrigerate, uncovered, for at least an hour, until the skin is taut and dry.

**6** Heat a deep skillet over a medium flame and add oil to a depth of 2cm. Brush the entire exterior of the bird with soy sauce, then dredge with water chestnut flour or cornstarch. When the oil reaches 170 degrees Celsius, carefully lower the chicken into the skillet. As the chicken fries, constantly ladle hot oil over the top. Turn it over and fry the other side, again ladling hot oil over the top. Fry for about eight minutes in total. Remove the bird from the skillet and heat the oil to 190 degrees. Briefly fry the bird on both sides, ladling oil over the top (the first frying is to heat the bird, the second is to crisp the skin). Drain on paper towels. Slice in half lengthwise before cutting into large pieces.

Serves 6-8 as part of a Chinese meal.

# QUAILS WITH ROASTED GARLIC, CARAMELISED LEMON, PETITS POIS AND CARROTS

## INGREDIENTS

1 head of garlic
60ml olive oil, divided
4 quails
4 sprigs fresh thyme
1 large lemon
30 grams unsalted butter
2 large shallots, minced
1 medium-sized carrot, peeled and diced
300 grams petits pois
100ml quail stock, made by simmering the quail
bones with about 200ml water for 45 minutes
1 1/2 tsp fresh thyme leaves
45ml cream
Fine sea salt and freshly ground black pepper

## METHOD

1 Cut off the two end joints of the quail wings, so only the drumette portion is left. Put each quail breast-side down on the cutting board, with the tail end closest to you. Gently work your fingertips between the flesh and backbone and start pulling them apart, taking care not to tear the thin flesh. Pull the meat away from the backbone down the entire length, all the way to the neck, and remove the bone. Feel around in the cavity for the rib bones and pull them out.

2 Turn the quail over so it's breast side-up. Working from the tail end of the bird, use a sharp paring knife to make a slit in the thin membrane at the breastbone, then use your fingertips to start separating the flesh from the breastbone, working carefully where the two sides of the breast come together because the flesh is very thin. Work as far down the breastbone as you can, then snap it off within the cavity and pull it out. Turn the bird around so the neck-side is facing you. Pull out the wishbone and collarbones from the cavity, using a paring knife to cut the tough tendons. Feel around the cavity for any bones you may have missed and remove them. When you're finished, the only bones in the bird should be the drumettes (on the wings) and the

drumstick and thigh bones. Season the quail cavities and skin with salt and pepper.

3 Preheat the oven to 220 degrees Celsius. Break the head of garlic into individual cloves, leaving the thin, papery skin intact. Drizzle the cloves with 20ml olive oil, wrap them loosely in aluminium foil and bake for about 30 minutes, or until tender. Cool the garlic to room temperature. Turn the oven up to 230 degrees. Quarter the lemon lengthwise and remove any seeds. Heat a small skillet over a medium-high flame until very hot. Add 10ml of olive oil and put the lemon quarters, cut-side down, in the skillet. Brown on one side, turn the lemons over and sear the other cut side. Cool to room temperature.

4 Stuff the cavity of each quail with one piece of lemon, two or three garlic cloves and a thyme sprig, then use kitchen string to truss the legs close to the body. Rub about 10ml of olive oil over the birds. Heat an oven-proof skillet until very hot. Place the quails, breast side-down in the skillet and sear over a high heat until medium brown, then turn them over and brown the other side. Put the skillet with the birds into the 230-degree oven and cook for about eight

minutes, or until the quails are done. Remove the trussing string from the quails when they're cooked.

**5** While the quails are cooking, heat the butter with 20ml olive oil. Add the shallots and cook until soft, then stir in the carrot, petits pois and thyme leaves. Stir in the quail stock and season with salt and pepper. Cover the pan partially with a lid and simmer until the vegetables are tender, stirring occasionally.

**6** Put the quails in the pan, drizzle the cream over them, then simmer until most of the liquid has evaporated. Serve immediately. Squeeze the lemon (from the cavity) over the birds. The roasted garlic cloves (once they've been squeezed from the papery skin) will be sweet and tender.

Serves 4.

# VEAL SWEETBREADS WITH BEURRE NOISETTE AND CAPERS

## INGREDIENTS

500 grams veal sweetbreads, thawed, if frozen
About 50ml fresh lemon juice
Fine sea salt and freshly ground black pepper
About 100 grams plain (all-purpose) flour, for dredging
Oil, for pan-frying
80 grams unsalted butter, at room temperature
2 heaped tbsp capers, drained
Lemon wedges, for serving

## METHOD

1 Rinse the sweetbreads, place them in a bowl and cover with cool water. Refrigerate for eight hours or longer, changing the water several times. Drain them, put them in a saucepan, cover with cold water and stir in the fresh lemon juice. Place over a medium flame, bring to the boil, then lower the heat and simmer for about 10 minutes (cook them for longer if they're large). Drain the sweetbreads, rinse them with cold water and soak in a bowl of iced water.

2 When the sweetbreads are cold, pull off and discard the thick membranes covering the glands and remove any veins and lumps of fat, leaving intact the thin membranes holding the pieces together. Place them on a paper-towel-lined tray, cover with more paper towels, then place another tray directly on top. Weigh down the top tray with fairly heavy items - cans of soup or water-filled saucepans - but don't crush them; you just want to compress the glands, not squash them flat. Refrigerate for a few hours.

3 Heat the butter in a small saucepan over a low fire until it melts, then continue cooking until it smells nutty and the milk solids at the bottom of the pan turn medium-brown (take care because the fat will splatter). Stir in the capers then keep the mixture warm.

4 Put the flour in a bowl, add about 3/4 teaspoon salt and as much ground pepper as you like, then combine thoroughly. Cut the sweetbreads on the diagonal into pieces about 1.5cm thick (if they're smaller glands - about 3cm in diameter - you can leave them whole). Pour oil into a skillet to a depth of about 5mm and heat over a medium-high flame. Dredge the sweetbread pieces in the flour and pan-fry on both sides in the hot oil until they're golden brown and crisp, then drain on paper towels.

5 Place the sweetbreads on plates. Spoon the butter and capers over and around the sweetbreads, add a lemon wedge to each portion and serve immediately.

Serves 6 as a starter, 3 as a main course.

# SALTED CARAMEL ICE-CREAM SUNDAES WITH BITTERSWEET CHOCOLATE SAUCE AND SWEET AND SALTY POPCORN

The recipe for the bittersweet chocolate sauce is from *Frozen Desserts* by Francisco J. Migoya.

This makes far more popcorn than you'll need for the sundaes, but the rest makes a good snack; just store in an airtight container and eat it quickly before it goes stale. You need an ice-cream maker for this dessert. The ice cream should be made in advance so it has time to harden.

## INGREDIENTS

FOR THE SALTED CARAMEL ICE CREAM
180 grams granulated sugar, divided
3 large egg yolks
1/2-3/4 tsp fine-grain sea salt
500ml cream
500ml whole milk
30ml dark rum

FOR THE BITTERSWEET CHOCOLATE SAUCE
55ml milk
110ml cream
55 grams glucose or corn syrup
165 grams bittersweet chocolate (with a cacao content of about 65 per cent), chopped
110ml water

FOR THE SWEET AND SALTY POPCORN
45ml cooking oil
60 grams popcorn kernels
50 grams granulated sugar
1/2 tsp fine-grain sea salt

## METHOD

1 Make the ice cream first so it has time to cool and then freeze. Put a fine sieve over a mixing bowl and place this next to the stove. Put 130 grams of sugar in a medium-sized saucepan and stir in about 40ml of water (the exact amount doesn't matter). Bring to the boil over a medium flame, then cover the pan with the lid and simmer for three minutes. Remove the lid and cook the sugar without stirring until it turns pale golden. Swirl the pan (but do not stir) so the sugar caramelises evenly, then cook to a medium-dark brown. Watch carefully, especially as it starts to darken.

2 While the sugar is cooking, heat the cream and milk in another pan. Bring to a simmer and turn off the heat. As soon as the caramel is ready, ladle in some of the hot cream/milk - take care because the caramel will splatter. Turn your face from the hot steam and protect your hand by wrapping it in a dishcloth. After gradually adding in all the milk/cream, stir the mixture over a low flame until smooth, then turn off the heat.

3 In a bowl, whisk the egg yolks with the salt and the remaining sugar until dissolved. Add a ladleful of the hot caramel mixture to the yolks and whisk immediately. Repeat twice, then pour this mixture into the saucepan containing the caramel and milk/cream.

4 Place over a low flame and stir constantly with a wooden spoon, making sure to cover the entire bottom of the pan as you stir. The mixture is ready when it coats the spoon and it leaves a track when you draw your finger across the spoon. Pour the custard through the sieve into the bowl and cool to room temperature, stirring often. Chill in the fridge until very cold, then stir in the rum. Process in an ice-cream maker according to the manufacturer's directions, then pack into a container and freeze until firm.

5 For the chocolate sauce, put the milk, cream and glucose or corn syrup in a pan, stir to combine then bring to the boil. Pour into a bowl over the chocolate and water and mix until smooth with an immersion blender or a whisk.

6 For the popcorn, put the oil in a large pan, add a few kernels and set it over a medium flame. Shake constantly until the kernels pop, then add the sugar and remaining popcorn and stir to coat. Cover the pan and shake constantly until the kernels pop. Sprinkle with the salt and stir to combine. Taste the popcorn and add more salt if needed.

Scoop the ice cream into bowls, add some popcorn, then drizzle with the chocolate sauce.

Serves 8-10.

# KOUIGN AMANN

Use top-quality salted butter for this pastry, which is a speciality of Brittany, France. Eat these rich treats warm out of the oven for afternoon tea.

## INGREDIENTS

### FOR THE DOUGH
275 grams bread flour
5 grams fine sea salt
5 grams instant yeast
175ml water (at 35 degrees Celsius)
10 grams salted butter, melted then cooled to tepid
A little cooking oil, for coating a mixing bowl
220 grams salted butter, chilled

### FOR ROLLING
Plain (all-purpose) flour
225 grams granulated sugar

### FOR THE TOPPING
20 grams melted salted butter
25 grams granulated sugar combined with 1 tsp fine sea salt

## METHOD

1 Put the bread flour, salt and yeast in the bowl of a food processor and pulse to combine. With the motor running, pour the water in a steady stream through the feed tube and add 10 grams of melted butter. Process for about 30 seconds to form a soft, damp, slightly sticky, dough. Transfer to a lightly oiled bowl, turn the dough over so the oiled side is on top, then cover with cling film and refrigerate for 30 minutes.

2 Cut the chilled butter into chunks and mix in the food processor until soft, but still cold. Shape it on a piece of parchment paper into a 15cm square.

3 Dust a work surface with plain flour. Roll out the dough to a 25cm square that's a little thinner at the corners. Place the butter square in the centre of the dough at a 45-degree angle and peel away the parchment. Fold the corners of the dough up and over the butter to enclose it securely. Press the dough firmly with the palm of your hand to flatten it slightly. Roll out the dough and butter packet into a 30cm by 20cm rectangle. Use a pastry brush to dust off the excess flour from the dough. Fold the top third of the dough towards the centre, brush off the excess flour, then fold the bottom third over the top so you have three even layers. Place the dough in a large ziplock bag and refrigerate for 30 minutes. Clean all the flour from the work surface, then liberally sprinkle it with sugar. Place the dough so one short edge is parallel to the edge of the work surface, then sprinkle more sugar over the dough. Roll it out to a 32cm by 20cm rectangle, adding more sugar if it sticks. Fold the dough into thirds (don't brush off the sugar), then refrigerate for 30 minutes.

4 Repeat the rolling and folding one more time, again using sugar on the work surface and the dough. The dough will be very damp, so you'll need to use more and more sugar to prevent it sticking to the work surface and rolling pin. Fold the dough into thirds, wrap it and refrigerate for 30 minutes.

5 Sprinkle the work surface with more sugar and roll the dough into a 32cm square (by this time, you should have used up all - or almost all - of the 225 grams of sugar). Use a pizza dough wheel to trim off the edges, then cut the dough into 16 8cm squares. Fold the corners of each square towards the centre so they're slightly overlapping,

and press firmly to make them adhere. Nestle each dough square into 6cm to 7cm muffin tins (or use pastry rings). Place on a baking tray (if using rings, lay a silicon baking mat on the tray first) and let the kouign amann rise until puffy.

6 Preheat the oven to 200 degrees. Brush melted butter on the surface of each kouign amann and sprinkle with some of the sugar-salt mixture. Bake at 200 degrees for 10 minutes then turn the heat to 180 degrees and bake until they're medium golden and firm on the surface but still tender at the centre (about 30 minutes in total). Remove from the muffin tins or rings while they're still hot. Serve them warm or cool. If the crust softens, they can be reheated at 180 degrees for about five minutes.

Makes 16.

# PINEAPPLE TARTS

In Singapore, pineapple tarts come in many shapes, from small rounds, or ovals, that are entirely pastry-encased, with only a small amount of jam inside, to two-layer cookies with jam at the centre. These tartlet-shaped pineapple tarts contain a lot more jam than you'll find in commercial offerings.

## INGREDIENTS

500 grams plain (all-purpose) flour
10 grams sugar
375 grams slightly softened butter
3/4 tsp fine sea salt
150ml iced water

### FOR THE PINEAPPLE JAM
Rough-flaked sea salt
1 large pineapple (weighing at least 1kg)
500 grams sugar
6-8 whole cloves
1 cinnamon stick (about 5cm long), broken into several pieces
Half a vanilla bean
50ml fresh lemon juice
Water, as needed

## METHOD

1 Cut the top and bottom of the pineapple, then remove the skin and eyes. Quarter the pineapple lengthwise and cut out and discard the core. Cut the pineapple into 1cm chunks and place them in a large colander. Sprinkle the fruit with salt and mix to coat it evenly. Leave for about an hour, mixing occasionally. Rinse the fruit thoroughly with cold water to wash away all of the salt - sample several pieces to make sure it doesn't taste salty. Drain the fruit, then weigh it - you should have at least 750 grams. If you have more or less than 750 grams of pineapple, adjust the amount of sugar proportionately (two parts sugar to three parts fruit by weight).

2 Put the fruit into a large, sturdy pan. Slit the piece of vanilla bean lengthwise and scrape out the seeds. Put the seeds and scraped-out pod into the pan, along with the sugar, cloves, cinnamon and about 150ml of water. Place the pan over a low flame and heat, stirring frequently, until all the sugar is dissolved. Continue to cook the ingredients over a low flame for about five hours, stirring frequently and adding water if necessary to prevent the jam from sticking to the pan. When it's ready, the fruit will be broken down into small pieces and the jam will be thick and deep golden brown. Stir in the lemon juice. Remove the vanilla pod and the pieces of cinnamon stick, ladle the jam into jars and cool completely.

3 Dissolve the salt in the iced water. In a large bowl, mix the flour with the sugar. Cut the butter into small chunks and add them to the flour mixture. Use your fingertips to combine all the ingredients and pinch the butter into smaller and smaller flour-coated pieces. When the mixture resembles coarse meal, drizzle the water over the ingredients. Mix with your hand until the dry ingredients are evenly moistened, then knead the dough lightly and briefly. Divide the dough into two even pieces, flatten each one into a disc, wrap in a double layer of cling film and refrigerate for at least an hour.

4 Pinch off 1.5cm chunks of dough and shape them into balls. Press the balls into tartlet pans about 3cm in diameter. The dough should be about 2mm thick at the sides and a little thinner at the base. Roll some of the scraps of dough about 2mm thick between two layers of cling film, then use a small pizza wheel to cut the dough into strands about 2mm wide and 2cm long. Refrigerate the tartlets and dough strands for about 30 minutes.

5 Preheat the oven to 180 degrees Celsius. Spoon some of the pineapple jam into each tartlet mould, making a mound at the centre. Put two strands of dough in a criss-cross shape over the jam. Place the tartlets on a tray and bake for about 10 minutes, or until they're golden brown. Cool before removing from the pans.

# MACARONS WITH SAKURA CREAM

The macaron shells are based on the technique in *Macaron* by Pierre Hermé. Buy pure icing sugar that doesn't contain any other ingredients. Sakura paste is sold at shops specialising in Japanese ingredients or baking supplies. If you can't find it, use sour-cherry jam.

## INGREDIENTS

150 grams icing (confectioner's) sugar
150 grams ground almonds
110 grams egg white, divided, at room temperature
1/4 tsp fine sea salt
150 grams granulated sugar
Red liquid food colouring

FOR THE SAKURA CREAM
Red liquid food colouring
240 grams double cream, chilled
Sakura paste, to taste
Granulated sugar, to taste

## METHOD

1 Put the ground almonds and icing sugar in a food processor and blend until the almonds are as fine as they can be and the icing sugar is no longer lumpy. Add 55 grams of egg white and process to a paste. Scrape the mixture into a large mixing bowl.

2 Put the remaining egg white into a medium-sized mixing bowl, with the salt ready nearby. Put the granulated sugar in a small saucepan, add 60ml of water and stir to dissolve. Bring to a simmer over a medium flame, then use a wet pastry brush to wash the sugar crystals from the sides of the pan. Cook the syrup without stirring until it reads 115 degrees Celsius on a candy thermometer. Immediately start whisking the egg white with a hand mixer and when it is frothy, add the salt. Watch the thermometer and when the syrup reaches 118 degrees, remove it from the heat and start pouring it in a steady stream into the egg white while mixing on medium speed. When all the syrup has been added, turn the mixer speed to high and whip the egg white until tepid. Mix a couple of drops of red food colouring into the whites. Add two-thirds of the whipped egg white into the almond-sugar mixture and mix until combined. Add the remaining white and fold it in. Stir for about 30 seconds. The consistency is right when you lift the spatula from the bowl and the mixture drips off, briefly remains on the surface and then slowly sinks into the remaining batter. Scrape the mixture into a large piping bag fitted with an 8mm tip. Pipe out the batter into 2.5cm circles onto a parchment-lined tray, leaving a little space between them so they have room to spread. Bang the tray firmly on the work surface to remove large air bubbles from the batter. Leave at room temperature to dry slightly.

3 Preheat the oven to 180 degrees. Bake the macarons (one tray at a time) for seven minutes, then lower the heat to 160 degrees and bake until done. If you're using a convection oven, the macarons will take about 10 more minutes. If it's a regular oven, they'll take a little longer and you'll need to turn the pan around halfway through. The surface of the macarons should darken only slightly; if they become too dark, lower the heat to 140 degrees. To check if the macarons are ready, touch the surface of one and jiggle it slightly; it should stand firm. Cool to room temperature, then use a metal spatula to remove the macarons from the tray.

4 Whisk the double cream with sakura paste, some sugar and a little food colouring to tint it pale pink. Sandwich the macarons together with the filling.

# ALAIN DUCASSE'S FINANCIERS

These little cakes were so named because of their rich ingredients - nuts and lots of butter - and from the traditional shape, which is said to resemble a bar of gold.

I've tried many recipes for financiers; this one - my favourite so far - comes from *Le Grand Livre de Cuisine d'Alain Ducasse: Desserts et Patisserie*. The recipe works best using commercial brands of ground nuts because the texture is fine and even.

## INGREDIENTS

220 grams unsalted butter
60 grams ground almonds or hazelnuts
60 grams plain (all-purpose) flour
1/4 tsp fine sea salt
180 grams icing sugar
160 grams egg white
1 tsp pure vanilla extract

## METHOD

1 Put the butter in a medium-sized saucepan and heat over a low-medium flame until it's melted. Continue to cook the butter - it will sizzle and pop until the moisture in it evaporates - until the milk solids at the bottom of the pan turn deep brown (this is called beurre noisette, or hazelnut butter). Pour the butter through a sieve into a bowl and discard the burnt solids; cool the butter until lukewarm.

2 Put the nuts, flour, salt and icing sugar in the food processor and process to combine. With the motor running, add the egg whites and vanilla through the feed tube. Pour in the butter and process briefly. Scrape the mixture into a bowl, cover with plastic wrap and refrigerate for at least three hours.

3 Preheat the oven to 200 degrees Celsius. Lightly spray financier moulds with pan coating. Fill the moulds three-quarters full with the chilled mixture and bake at 200 degrees until the financiers have risen slightly and are fragrant, firm to the touch, golden brown on top and medium brown at the edges (about 10-15 minutes, depending on the size of the moulds). Allow to cool slightly before removing the financiers from the moulds; they are best when eaten within about four hours. The batter can be stored in the fridge for a week.

Makes about 30.

# CHAMPAGN

You don't need to use grande
(although if you do use a top

Sabayon requires constant
want a burned crust on the sa

## INGREDIENTS

6 large egg yolks, at room t
1/4 tsp fine sea salt
70 grams granulated sugar
180ml champagne brut, at
Fresh strawberries, raspber

# GINGERBREAD PEOPLE

This recipe is based on one in *Rose's Christmas Cookies* by Rose Levy Beranbaum. The dough can also be used to make gingerbread houses and other shapes.

FOR THE GINGERBREAD DOUGH
**170 grams unsalted butter**
**150 grams dark brown sugar**
**1/4 tsp fine sea salt**
**1 tsp baking soda**
**2 tsp ground ginger**
**1 tsp ground cinnamon**
**1/2 tsp grated nutmeg**
**1/4 tsp ground cloves**
**1 large egg**
**160 grams molasses**
**425 grams plain (all-purpose) flour, plus**
**extra for the work surface**

FOR THE ROYAL ICING
**90 grams egg white**
**460 grams icing sugar, sieved**

1 Make the gingerbread dough at least two hours before rolling it. Beat the butter with the sugar until it's light and fluffy. Add the salt, baking soda, ginger, cinnamon, nutmeg and cloves and beat well to combine. Turn the mixer speed to low, add the egg and mix until combined, then stir in the molasses. Scrape the bowl and beaters with a rubber spatula. Add all the flour at once and stir to combine. Divide the dough into two parts, shape them into flat discs and wrap well in cling film. Refrigerate for at least two hours.

2 Preheat the oven to 180 degrees Celsius. On a well-floured work surface, roll out the dough so it's about 3mm thick. Cut out the shapes using gingerbread men and women cookie cutters. The dough is very soft so the shapes can be difficult to move once they have been cut out. Carefully transfer them to a baking tray lined with parchment paper. Bake at 180 degrees until the cookies are fragrant and firm to the touch. Allow to cool before icing them.

3 To make the royal icing, put the egg white and icing sugar in a clean, dry bowl. Use clean, dry beaters to stir on low speed until the sugar is moistened. Turn the mixer speed to medium and beat until the ingredients are thick and glossy: when you touch the mixture it should form a peak that curves slightly. If you're not planning to use the icing immediately, scrape it into a small bowl and put a damp paper towel directly on the surface; if it softens, re-beat it before using. Put the icing into a paper cornet (or a piping bag fitted with a 2mm plain tip) and pipe decorations on the gingerbread people. Leave until the icing is hard. If not serving immediately, pack the gingerbread into airtight containers.

# CHOCOLATE BUTTER CRUNCH

I've tried many butter crunch recipes and methods and finally found one that's dependable. Unfortunately, this means not making it on rainy or humid days because the butter crunch absorbs moisture in the air. Fortunately, Hong Kong's winter days are dry, but to ensure the recipe is a success, you might want to consider turning on the air-conditioner and de-humidifiers. You need a candy thermometer to make this.

I usually temper the chocolate so it maintains a nice sheen, even at room temperature. The process, which involves melting, cooling and warming the chocolate, is time-consuming and doesn't always work, even though I've done it many times. To get around this, melt the chocolate, spread it on the butter crunch and cover with lots of nuts. The finished product should be stored in the fridge.

Butter crunch is also known as toffee or butter crackle. The yield is large, so halve the recipe if you wish. Pack the butter crunch in colourful, tissue paper-lined airtight tins.

## INGREDIENTS

250 grams sliced almonds, divided
250 grams unsalted butter
350 grams granulated sugar
30 grams corn syrup
500 grams bittersweet chocolate (don't use unsweetened), finely chopped

## METHOD

1 Spray a large, flat baking tray with pan coating, then line as smoothly as possible with aluminium foil. Lightly spray the foil and a metal spatula.

2 Toast the almonds in an 180 degree Celsius oven until light brown. Cool the nuts completely. Finely chop about 75 grams of the nuts and coarsely chop the remainder.

3 Melt the butter in a medium-sized heavy pan. Add the sugar and corn syrup and stir to dissolve. Dip a pastry brush in water and brush the sugar crystals onto the sides of the pan (this prevents the sugar from crystallising later). Do not stir the sugar again until it's time to add the nuts.

Attach a candy thermometer to the side of the pan and let the mixture boil until it reaches 150 degrees Celsius. Immediately stir in the 75 grams of finely chopped nuts, then pour the mixture onto the prepared tray, using the oiled spatula to spread the mixture into a thin layer. Let it cool completely.

4 Melt the chocolate in a microwave on high power, stirring every 30 seconds until it is about 80 per cent melted, then let the residual heat melt the remaining pieces. You can also melt it over a double boiler (stir frequently), taking care not to allow moisture into the chocolate. If you used a double boiler, dry the bottom of the bowl with a tea towel.

5 Use paper towels to soak up any oil on the surface of the butter crunch, then spread half the melted chocolate on top and sprinkle with half the roughly chopped nuts. Chill until the chocolate is firm. Place a sheet of aluminium foil on top, put a second baking tray on top of the foil and turn it over so the unglazed side is facing up. Peel off the layer of aluminium foil and blot up any fat on the surface of the butter crunch. Spread the remaining chocolate on top and sprinkle with the remaining nuts. Cool completely before breaking into uneven pieces.

# ACKNOWLEDGEMENTS

A lifetime of eating and cooking went into the development of this book. Through their delicious meals, my parents, grandparents and favourite uncle, Gene, instilled in me an appreciation of good food. For that I can't thank them enough.

Many thanks also to the chefs, cooks and restaurateurs with whom I've worked over the years, in particular Richard Feldman, who has the ability to make me laugh even when we're both feeling overworked; and Paul Hsu of Elite Concepts and Clayton Parker, now of Eclipse Management. Paul and Clayton hired me as a pastry chef – sight unseen – and brought me to Hong Kong from New York in 1993.

A million thanks to Charles Anderson and Hedley Thomas, who, in 1997, were Features Editor and Deputy Features Editor respectively of the *South China Morning Post*. I'd been writing for them as a freelance journalist for only six months when they took me to lunch to ask whether I was interested in becoming the SCMP's Food and Wine Editor. I couldn't say yes quickly enough.

Thanks to the editors and sub-editors with whom I've worked since then, in particular Winnie Chung, Desiree Au, Victoria Finlay, Mark Footer, Rachael Barker, Meera Ganesan, Daniel Jeffreys, Susan Sams and Thong Yoke-mei, who have tried, to the best of their abilities, to make me sound intelligent on paper. Special thanks to Charmaine Chan for the hard work that went into editing this book, and to Steve Ellul, who designed it. Thanks, too, to this newspaper's marketing team, who initiated the project.

The chefs and restaurateurs who contributed some of the recipes in the book have been remarkably tolerant, allowing me into their kitchens with a photographer and putting up with my incessant questions about quantities, ingredients and techniques. It's been wonderfully enlightening watching them demonstrate their cooking skills.

I count myself lucky to have friends all over the world who share my love of eating and who take great joy in dining out, cooking for each other ... and coming to visit bearing edible gifts purchased on their travels.

Thanks to Peter Chang, Lambda Li, Jessie Ng, Janine Cheung, CSY, Sherman Chan, David Lai, Dave Kunin, Celine Flamain, Deirdre and Nico, Amy and Alex, Yvonne Teh, Rose Leng, Eddie and Sophia, Meei and Francois, Loke See-wah, Supapohn Kanwerayotin, Annabel and Russell, the Diestel family, the Chu family, Jan and Keith, Rey and Louise, Judy Yu, Josh Tse, Wilson Fok, Eileen Jung and Fuchsia Dunlop.

Thanks to the food stylists (Rachael Macchiesi, Vivian Herijanto and Nellie Ming Lee) and photographers (Jason Bonello, Jonathan Wong, Patrick Poon, KY Cheng and Nora Tam) who have made my food look appetising in this book and in the *Post Magazine*.

And endless thanks to my husband, Nigel, who tolerates – and sometimes encourages – my obsession with food.

This book is in memory of my grandparents, who cooked for me, and Charles Anderson, who believed in me.

# INDEX

**A**

Abalone, sautéed sliced, with onion and wild mushrooms, Cuisine Cuisine's **86**

Above & Beyond's oolong tea-smoked duck eggs with black truffle paste **146**

Aebleskivers **14**

Affogato **118**

Ajo blanco with grape sorbet and croutons **132**

Albondigas soup **20**

Almond soup, Chinese, Fook Lam Moon's **60**

Ammo's angel hair pasta with uni, tomatoes and garlic chips **92**

Apricot, vanilla-poached, raspberry and Greek yogurt parfaits with lemon and muscovado sugar crumble **114**

**B**

Balinese chopped purple cabbage and chicken salad, Heirloom's **26**

Bamboo clams, grilled, with garlic, butter and parsley **84**

Banana cream pie **116**

Beancurd
  Mapo doufu, Bistro Jinli's **52**
  Pipa doufu, Celebrity Cuisine's **152**

Beef
  Albondigas soup **20**
  Honeycomb tripe with parmesan cheese **54**
  Macchiesi family spaghetti with polpetti **58**
  Oxtail braised in red wine **56**
  Tortas with spiced flank steak, crushed black beans and avocado **50**
  Yukhoe **112**

Beets
  Grilled quails with baby spinach, arugula, beetroot and mustard dressing **72**
  Heirloom, with yogurt and cream cheese espuma, Mandarin Grill's **134**

Bistro Jinli's mapo doufu **52**

Bread pudding with crème anglaise and whisky sauce **64**

**C**

Cabbage
  Choucroute garnie **102**
  Kimchi **30**
  Balinese chopped purple cabbage and chicken salad, Heirloom's **26**

Caprice's crab tiramisu with fruit and tandoori spices **142**

Caramel
  Chocolate and salted caramel tarts **120**
  Salted caramel ice-cream sundaes with bittersweet chocolate sauce and sweet and salty popcorn **160**

Celebrity Cuisine's pipa doufu **152**

Cépage's miso-marinated black cod in hoba leaf with pickled young Japanese ginger **148**

Chairman's, The, spare ribs with preserved plums and caramelised black vinegar **100**

Champagne sabayon with fresh berries **170**

Chawanmushi with black truffle paste and uni, Sushi Kuu's **128**

Cherry pie, deep-dish, with flaky crust **122**

Cherry tomato and ricotta tart with whole-wheat and olive-oil crust **76**

Chicken
  Balinese chopped purple cabbage and chicken salad, Heirloom's **26**
  Karaage **44**
  Nor mai gai **154**
  Smoked, Kin's Kitchen's **110**
  Spiral curry puffs **106**
  Wings, Thai-style **46**
  Yellow earth, Yin Yang's **48**

Chickpeas with kabocha, curry and yogurt **70**

Chocolate
  Bittersweet chocolate sauce, with salted caramel ice cream sundaes and sweet and salty popcorn **160**
  Butter crunch **174**

Clams, bamboo, grilled, with garlic, butter and parsley **84**

Crab
  Crab, asparagus and saffron tarts **144**
  Soft-shell crab salad with candied orange peel, toasted hazelnuts and citrus dressing **136**
  Tiramisu, with fruit and tandoori spices, Caprice's **142**

Cuisine Cuisine's sautéed sliced abalone with onion and wild mushrooms **86**

Curry-dusted shrimp and scallop skewers with mango, coconut and kaffir lime salsa **82**

Curry puffs, spiral **106**

**E**

Eggs
  Chawanmushi with black truffle paste and uni, Sushi Kuu's **128**
  Oolong tea-smoked duck eggs with black truffle paste, Above & Beyond's **146**
  Scotch **96**

**F**

Fan Tang's stir-fried lettuce with shrimp paste in clay pot **32**

Fish
  Citrus, fennel and aquavit-cured salmon with lemon-horseradish sour cream **140**
  Miso-marinated black cod in hoba leaf with pickled young Japanese ginger, Cépage's **148**
  Salt-baked fish with uni rouille, On Lot 10's **94**
  Seared tuna with corn, avocado salsa and ikura **88**
  Snapper with baby spinach, Otto e Mezzo's **138**

Financiers, Alain Ducasse's **168**

Focaccia with pancetta, caramelised onions and rosemary **68**

Fook Lam Moon's Chinese almond soup **60**

Fritto misto **36**

Fruit
  Banana cream pie **116**
  Braised pomelo skin with shrimp roe, Tim's Kitchen **34**
  Champagne sabayon with fresh berries **170**
  Citrus, fennel and aquavit-cured salmon with lemon-horseradish sour cream **140**

Cherry pie, deep-dish, with flaky crust **122**

Crab tiramisu with fruit and tandoori spices, Caprice's **142**

Curry-dusted shrimp and scallop skewers with mango, coconut and kaffir lime salsa **82**

Deep-dish cherry pie with flaky crust **122**

Pineapple tarts **164**

Raspberry, vanilla-poached apricot and Greek yogurt parfaits with lemon and muscovado sugar crumble **114**

Soft-shell crab salad with candied orange peel, toasted hazelnuts and citrus dressing **136**

Spare ribs with preserved plums and caramelised black vinegar, The Chairman's **100**

Summer pudding **62**

Watermelon, tomato and feta or goat cheese salad **24**

**G**

Gingerbread people **172**

**H**

He Jiang's sliced pork with chilli and garlic sauce **74**

Heirloom's Balinese chopped purple cabbage and chicken salad **26**

**I**

Il Posto 97's octopus carpaccio with olive oil, sticky balsamic and sweet paprika **80**

**K**

Kabocha
  Soup with ginger and curry, roasted **18**
  Chickpeas with kabocha, curry and yogurt **70**

Kimchi
  Cabbage **30**
  Pancakes **78**

Kin's smoked chicken **110**

Kouign amann **162**

**L**

Langoustines, salt-roasted, with roasted cherry tomatoes, white wine, arugula and squid-ink pasta **150**

Lettuce, stir-fried, with shrimp paste in clay pot, Fan Tang's **32**

**M**

Macarons with sakura cream **166**

Macchiesi family spaghetti with polpetti **58**

Mandarin Grill's heirloom beets with yogurt and cream cheese espuma **134**

Mushroom soup with truffle oil and mushroom toast **130**

Mushrooms and truffles
  Abalone, sautéed sliced, with onion and wild mushrooms, Cuisine Cuisine's **86**
  Chawanmushi with black truffle paste and uni, Sushi Kuu's **128**
  Fried Vietnamese spring rolls **104**
  Mushroom soup with truffle oil and mushroom toast **130**
  Oolong tea-smoked duck eggs with black truffle paste, Above & Beyond's **146**

Stir-fried rice vermicelli with belacan, pork belly and shrimp **40**
Mussels with potatoes, peppers and rouille **42**

**N**
Nasi lemak with spicy prawns **90**
Noodles and pasta
  Angel hair with uni, tomatoes and garlic chips, Ammo's **92**
  Macchiesi family spaghetti with polpetti **58**
  Salt-roasted langoustines with roasted cherry tomatoes, white wine, arugula and squid-ink pasta **150**
  Stir-fried rice vermicelli with belacan, pork belly and shrimp **40**
Nor mai gai **154**

**O**
Octopus carpaccio with olive oil, sticky balsamic and sweet paprika, Il Posto 97's **80**
On Lot 10's salt-baked fish with uni rouille **94**
Otto e Mezzo's snapper with baby spinach **138**
Oxtail braised in red wine **56**

**P**
Pigeons with green peas, morels, butter-roasted Japanese sweet potatoes and baby taro **108**
Pineapple tarts **164**
Polenta with bacon, shrimp and chives **38**
Pomelo skin, braised, with shrimp roe, Tim's Kitchen **34**
Pork
  Albondigas soup **20**
  Choucroute garnie **102**
  Focaccia with pancetta, caramelised onions and rosemary **68**
  Fried Vietnamese spring rolls **104**
  Macchiesi family spaghetti with polpetti **58**
  Nor mai gai **154**
  Pan-fried buns filled with pork and chives **16**
  Polenta with bacon, shrimp and chives **38**
  Savoury tong yuen **22**
  Scotch eggs **96**
  Stir-fried rice vermicelli with belacan, pork belly and shrimp **40**
  Schnitzel, with potato salad **98**
  Sliced, with chilli and garlic sauce, He Jiang's **74**
  Spare ribs with preserved plums and caramelised black vinegar, The Chairman's **100**
  Vietnamese fried spring rolls **104**
Potatoes
  Mussels with potatoes, peppers and rouille **42**
  Pigeons with green peas, morels, butter-roasted Japanese sweet potatoes and baby taro **108**
  Pork schnitzel with potato salad **98**
  Spiral curry puffs **106**

**Q**
Quails
  Grilled, with baby spinach, arugula, beetroot and mustard dressing **72**
  With roasted garlic, caramelised lemon, petits pois and carrots **156**

**R**
Raspberry, vanilla-poached apricot and Greek yogurt parfaits with lemon and muscovado sugar crumble **114**
Rice
  Nasi lemak with spicy prawns **90**
  Nor mai gai **154**
  Rice vermicelli stir-fried with belacan, pork belly and shrimp **40**
  Roasted kabocha soup with ginger and curry **18**

**S**
Salad
  Balinese chopped purple cabbage and chicken salad, Heirloom's **26**
  Pork schnitzel with potato salad **98**
  Soft-shell crab salad with candied orange peel, toasted hazelnuts and citrus dressing **136**
  Spinach and garlic shrimp salad **28**
  Watermelon, tomato and feta or goat cheese salad **24**
Salmon, citrus, fennel and aquavit-cured, with lemon-horseradish sour cream **140**
Scallops
  Curry-dusted shrimp and scallop skewers with mango, coconut and kaffir lime salsa **82**
  XO sauce **126**
Shakshuka **12**
Shrimp and prawns
  Curry-dusted shrimp and scallop skewers with mango, coconut and kaffir lime salsa **82**
  Fried Vietnamese spring rolls **104**
  Fritto misto **36**
  Nasi lemak with spicy prawns **90**
  Polenta with bacon, shrimp and chives **38**
  Spinach and garlic shrimp salad **28**
  Stir-fried rice vermicelli with belacan, pork belly and shrimp **40**
  XO sauce **126**
Soft-shell crab salad with candied orange peel, toasted hazelnuts and citrus dressing **136**
Soup
  Ajo blanco with grape sorbet and croutons **132**
  Albondigas soup **20**
  Almond soup, Chinese, Fook Lam Moon's **60**
  Mushroom soup with truffle oil and mushroom toast **130**
  Roasted kabocha soup with ginger and curry **18**
  Savoury tong yuen **22**
Spare ribs with preserved plums and caramelised black vinegar, The Chairman's **100**
Spaghetti with polpetti, Macchiesi family **58**
Spinach and garlic shrimp salad **28**

Spiral curry puffs **106**
Spring rolls, fried, Vietnamese **104**
Summer pudding **62**
Sushi Kuu's chawanmushi with black truffle paste and uni **128**
Sweetbreads, veal, with beurre noisette and capers **158**

**T**
Tarts
  Cherry tomato and ricotta tart with whole-wheat and olive-oil crust **76**
  Chocolate and salted caramel tarts **120**
  Crab, asparagus and saffron tarts **144**
  Pineapple tarts **164**
Thai-style chicken wings **46**
Tim's Kitchen's braised pomelo skin with shrimp roe **34**
Tomatoes
  Angel hair pasta with uni, tomatoes and garlic chips, Ammo's **92**
  Cherry tomato and ricotta tart with whole-wheat and olive-oil crust **76**
  Salt-roasted langoustines with roasted cherry tomatoes, white wine, arugula and squid-ink pasta **150**
  Shakshuka **12**
  Watermelon, tomato and feta or goat cheese salad **24**
Tong yuen, savoury **22**
Tortas with spiced flank steak, crushed black beans and avocado **50**
Tripe, honeycomb, with parmesan cheese **54**
Tuna, seared, with corn, avocado salsa and ikura **88**

**U**
Uni
  Angel hair pasta with uni, tomatoes and garlic chips, Ammo's **92**
  Chawanmushi with black truffle paste and uni, Sushi Kuu's **128**
  Salt-baked fish with uni rouille, On Lot 10's **94**

**V**
Veal sweetbreads with beurre noisette and capers **158**
Vietnamese fried spring rolls **104**

**W**
Watermelon, tomato and feta or goat cheese salad **24**

**X**
XO sauce **126**

**Y**
Yin Yang's yellow earth chicken **48**
Yogurt
  Chickpeas with kabocha, curry and yogurt **70**
  Heirloom beets with yogurt and cream cheese espuma, Mandarin Grill's **134**
  Raspberry, vanilla-poached apricot and Greek yogurt parfaits with lemon and muscovado sugar crumble **114**
Yukhoe **112**

Published By:
South China Morning Post Publishers Limited
Morning Post Centre
22 Dai Fat Street
Tai Po Industrial Estate
New Territories, Hong Kong


Printed By:
Regal Printing Limited
11/F Wyler Centre Phase II
192-200 Tai Lin Pai Road
Kwai Chung
New Territories, Hong Kong